Tahquamenon Country
A Look at Its Past

IN MEMORIAM

Charles Sprague Taylor
1920-1976

Tahquamenon Country
A Look at Its Past

Sprague Taylor

with original illustrations by
Nick Eggenhofer

East Lansing

Michigan State University Press
Historical Society of Michigan

⊗ The paper used in this publication meets the minimum requirements
of ANSI/NISO Z39.48-1992 (R 1997) (Permanence of Paper).

 Michigan State University Press
East Lansing, Michigan 48823-5245

 The Historical Society of Michigan
East Lansing, Michigan 48823
hsm@hsmichigan.org

Printed and bound in the United States of America.

14 13 12 11 10 09 08   1 2 3 4 5 6 7 8 9 10

ISBN: 978-0-87013-833-1

LIBRARY OF CONGRESS CATALOGING-IN-PUBLICATION DATA

Taylor, Charles Sprague.
Tahquamenon country : a look at its past / Sprague Taylor; with original
illustrations by Nick Eggenhofer.
p. cm.
Originally published: Ann Arbor : Historical Society of Michigan, 1991.
Includes bibliographical references and index.
ISBN 978-0-87013-833-1 (pbk. : alk. paper)   1. Upper Peninsula
(Mich.)—History, Local.   2. Tahquamenon River Region (Mich.)—
History, Local.   3. Upper Peninsula (Mich.)—Social life and customs.
4. Tahquamenon River Region (Mich.)—Social life and customs.
I. Title.
F572.N8T39 2008
977.4'925—dc22
2008008749

Cover design by Sharp Des!gns, Inc., Lansing, Michigan
Cover photograph is by David Lubbers and is used with permission.

g green Michigan State University Press is a member of the Green
press Press Initiative and is committed to developing and
INITIATIVE
encouraging ecologically responsible publishing practices. For more
information about the Green Press Initiative and the use of recycled
paper in book publishing, please visit *www.greenpressinitiative.org*.

Visit Michigan State University Press on the World Wide Web at:
www.msupress.msu.edu

Sprague Taylor

The *Hulbert* from Spater's Landing.

Contents

SURVEYOR

I measure grounds of men's laments
And am called because a neighbor's fence
Is quite within my compassing.

A needle moored to earth's transgress,
From moving pole to man's trespass,
Lies in this box; I shift it free

And tripoded, it will be
A circumbient arc, wherein
I stand,
A boundary-man, aimed at
needle's land.

If I could make one client
pause,
It would be to attend:
At times the line is not
where it ought to be,
Sorry, my friend,
But where it was, and I
mean just where it was.

Sprague Taylor ~ 1975

Introduction to the 2008 Edition

Much of Michigan's history is not contained in the grand stories of great personages involved in epic accomplishments, although that is often the level at which it is left to the ages. Rather our state's histories—and, for that matter, the histories of the world and even our own families—are in truth of a local scale and in minute detail, so local and so minute that they often go unnoticed and, unfortunately, unappreciated. But together, those "histories" are the true substance of its fabric. And so it is with Sprague Taylor's *Tahquamenon Country.*

—Publisher's Note, 1991

The Historical Society of Michigan in conjunction with the Michigan State University Press is pleased to reissue *Tahquamenon Country: A Look at it Past,* by Sprague Taylor. Originally published by the Society in 1991, Taylor's work represents a unique contribution to the historical scholarship of this unique area of the Upper Peninsula. To this day, there is a relative dearth of history written on Michigan's northern peninsula and its eastern half. There is even less that delves into Tahquamenon. The eastern Upper Peninsula lacks the intrigue of the copper and iron mines, and most of the other books about the region focus on historical landmarks such as the Mackinac Bridge, Sault Ste. Marie, or shipping on the Great Lakes.

Taylor's unique and perceptive story contains a wealth of historical information. Though written over a quarter of a century ago, this culmination of a lifetime spent collecting and documenting the rich history of Tahquamenon area of Michigan is still a strong Michigan history volume. Since *Tahquamenon Country* first appeared, there has been consistent demand for this book, and we are pleased to reissue it and bring this seminal work to a new generation of historians.

Larry J. Wagenaar

Introduction

There's something about a river ...

From the huge Mississippi to the small stream which has barely
enough water to float a canoe, rivers have a fascination which
is impossible to resist. The early French explorers who first
dipped their paddles into the waters of the Mississippi were
responding to the same impulses that seize today's recreational
canoeist - the irresistible urge to find out what is around the next
bend. The river is an enticing force which lures one on. One
experiences that fascination by merely sitting on the banks of the
river as its powerful current sweeps onward toward the sea.
Where will that water be tomorrow? Next week? Toss a chip into
the water. Perhaps it will be washed ashore in a few hours;
perhaps it will continue its voyage on for days and weeks and
even months. Stand by a waterfall or a river in spring flood and

feel the tremendous and fearful power of that current as it tosses huge logs about and jostles large boulders on its bed. Sit by a river and feel its hypnotic effect; it will hold you and draw you into a pensive trance.

Rivers were the highways for explorers, then trappers and hunters, then settlers. What must have been the feelings of those early French explorers who first gazed upon the mighty Mississippi? Where did it come from? Where did it go? Could they have envisioned that in little more than a century this broad expanse of water would be a busy highway, carrying settlers to new homes, bringing supplies to them, and taking their products to market? It is not likely that these early visitors could have imagined the river which inspired Mark Twain to create his great literature.

Rivers are full of history. Sitting on the shores of the serene Ohio of today, one can call up a picture of a busier day when steamboats, keelboats, and rafts dotted the surface of the river. The raft floating by with a crude cabin in the center, a man at the sweep, and his wife and children nearby, was bearing its passengers toward a new home in Missouri or Arkansas. Its cargo was the raft itself, made of hewn timbers cut and shaped by the family up river in West Virginia, Pennsylvania, or Ohio. Upon reaching the promised land, the pioneer could either sell his timber to acquire money for the purchase of land or he could use the timbers to build a new home. So much history in a river! The Platte River marked a trail which pioneers followed to settle the Pacific coast; the American River yielded those yellow pebbles which attracted a multitude of settlers to California; and the list could go on and on.

Rivers attracted villages, cities and towns. The number of cities with the word "Rapids" as part of their names is a reminder that rivers have power which may be utilized for the benefit of humankind. Sawmills, gristmills and factories which draw their power from the rivers attracted workers, merchants, families, and thus created cities.

The Tahquamenon is no Mississippi, Ohio or Missouri. It is not the largest river in Michigan. The Saginaw has the largest watershed; and the Grand winds its way from the southernmost part of Jackson County to Lake Michigan at Grand Haven. These rivers have helped to distribute a string of towns along their courses; and their seasonal overflowings over the centuries have created rich fields, which the farmers till. The Tahquamenon has not distinguished itself in these respects; yet it has its group of admirers, its own cadre of those who see in this river all that the historians of the Ohio and Mississippi see and more.

Charles Sprague Taylor was such an admirer of the Tahquamenon. The reader of his book will visualize him sitting on the river bank watching the water flow by, thinking and dreaming. He paddled a canoe over its course and tramped along its banks. He experienced the thrill of coming around a bend and seeing a family of ducklings following their mother, a deer drinking at the river bank, and beaver or a mink, and on occasion a black bear. To Sprague (as he was known to his friends) his was a special world in which he was content. He enjoyed the re-awakening of the earth in spring, the flourishing of nature in the summer, the brilliant colors of fall and the quiet solitude of winter. He knew the Tahquamenon in all its seasons.

At an early age he became curious about the past history of the Tahquamenon. He collected and read all that he could about the natives who had once made this river their thoroughfare. He read anthropological studies which revealed to him the habits and customs of early inhabitants of the area; and he could conjure up images of these natives gathering, hunting and fishing. The setting was there, minus the towering pines; all that was needed was the imagination to restore these early people to their natural setting.

Sprague sought out information about the early European explorers, read the Jesuit accounts of these early natives, and he read early missionary reports, correspondence and biographies. He visited libraries and wrote letters; and in doing so located historical accounts which had lain unread for more than a century. While reading the Rev. Abel Bingham papers at the Clarke Historical Library, Sprague found references to reports which Bingham had sent to Baptist missionary societies in New York City and Boston. Upon discovering that these organizations were still in existence, he wrote to them, learned that they had reports and correspondence from Abel Bingham, and gained access to these records.

He read Schoolcraft's books pertinent to the area and his correspondence in the Library of Congress, extracting any reference to the Tahquamenon. Here again he found clues to other collections and pursued them to find even more accounts of visits to this area. He was both a scholar and a detective.

Sprague had an advantage when it came to the logging period which was of considerable significance in the Tahquamenon region. He was born into a family which was associated with the lumbering industry and he also had the opportunity to talk with old-timers who had worked in the woods, some of whom had records or old photographs which they shared with him.

He became a competent photographer and not only made many pictures of the area but also copied old photographs. He collected printed materials about the area and always checked them carefully for accuracy. The Tahquamenon, however, was not his sole interest in life; he also collected books and enjoyed literature as well as history.

Charles Sprague Taylor was born at Newberry, Michigan, on February 5, 1920. His parents were living at Trout Lake; but Mrs. Taylor had come to Newberry by train to stay at the home of the midwife who delivered the baby. Charles was the son of Charles and Evelyn Sprague Taylor. His father was a lumberman and a former bank clerk. His mother had been a school teacher.

In 1926, after five years in camps and two more children, the family moved to nearby Hulbert, Michigan, where students could attend school through the tenth grade. In 1934 Sprague went to Sault Ste. Marie to complete the eleventh and twelfth grades, rooming with the superintendent of schools for Chippewa County.

He was graduated from the Sault High School at the age of 16, winning the cup for outstanding student. In high school he had participated in debate and was the high school reporter for the city newspaper; and he was elected president of the senior class. Upon graduation from high school, he attended Ferris Institute, where he particularly enjoyed composition and journalism; and he worked on the college paper. On December 8, 1941, the day after the attack upon Pearl Harbor, Sprague enlisted in the United States Army and was sent to Officers Candidate School at Fort Lee, where he was commissioned and assigned to the Quartermaster Corps. He rose to the rank of Captain.

Sprague's father spent most of his lifetime as a timber dealer, an occupation which enabled Sprague to accompany his father to logging sites and pulpwood cutting areas. On many occasions Sprague and his father hiked through the woods looking for land which contained timber for future production. When Sprague returned from World War II, he joined his father as an active partner in Taylor Forest Products and continued the business after his father's retirement.

Sprague's interest in the history of the Tahquamenon grew as he worked in the lumber industry, traveling the trails and old tote roads and tributaries of the Tahquamenon, Shelldrake and Two Hearted river systems. He interviewed old-timers, checked the accuracy of earlier printed accounts of the area, and followed every lead by correspondence or interview.

In his last years Sprague spent many hours bringing together his research notes, interviews and observations into a book which he expected to publish. Unfortunately, a series of heart attacks forced him to leave the lumber business; and an attack on January 29, 1976, caused his death.

Sprague was married to Carol Copeland, a native of Emmet County, whom he met when they were students at Ferris Institute. They had one son, Charles G. Taylor, whose photographs appear throughout his father's book.

The manuscript of this book, *Tahquamenon Country: A Look at Its Past*, has been made available to the Historical Society of Michigan by Carol Copeland Taylor. With the manuscript were many fine photographs of people and places collected by Sprague Taylor and a number of excellent photographs taken by Sprague and his son. The noted artist and illustrator Nick Eggenhofer drew sketches of scenes in the Tahquamenon area both past and present.

The principal emphasis of the book is on the native history of the region together with the legends which have been passed on by these first inhabitants of the river valley and on the lumbering period. That so much information about this area and period is from personal accounts may surprise the reader. The lumbering period is drawn mostly from the personal interviews with people who were there, although official records were studied for statistics and whatever else they may have offered. Anecdotes and legends enliven the narrative.

One aspect of the lumbering industry in the Tahquamenon that is seldom encountered in other logging literature is the preparation of logs for shipment to England. Men with broadaxes shaped the timbers, squaring them on all four sides so that they might be stowed more compactly in the holds of ships and on deck. These were called "waney board timber" by the lumberjacks. The timbers were then rafted to Quebec for shipment to England.

The author's sources, for the most part, are identified within the text, rather than in footnotes. A complete bibliography at the end of the book further identifies them.

John Cumming
Mt. Pleasant, Michigan

Preface

Newberry, Michigan, 1975

It is now over forty years since I first traveled, bow-paddle in a canoe, down the river. The Tahquamenon excites in me still some of the boyish wonder and anticipatory gladness I knew then. I feel lucky to have lived beside it, to have had innumerable chances to explore the backwaters and headstreams that thread its basin. I have had time to pursue, here among fellow villagers and elsewhere, as fancy and a questing nature took me, the intermittent, absorbing research for understanding that underlies and (I would hope) informs these pages.

This is not intended to be a complete, documented local history. The aim has been to piece together, in a rough, chronological order, some of the notes and impressions accumulated during a spare-time interest in a trio of adjoining river systems: Tahquamenon, Shelldrake (or Betsy) and Two

Sprague Taylor, 1930.

Hearted. Like any main waterway, the Tahquamenon had a story of its own. My emphasis here is on that story, and especially on those aspects of it that reflect what must be essentially a woodsman's viewpoint.

I am aware that, in the fragments of the Tahquamenon story that follow, important elements have been scanted arbitrarily. I did not mean to do this when I set out, of course; but gradually, as my fondness for the things and people of the woods took over, I allowed it to prevail, content to travel light and to leave to others such matters as socioeconomic forces or political beginnings.

The assembling of certain data for this book was made easier by the late William B. Fretz, whose obliging interest in Tahquamenon history extended through his fifty years as publisher and editor of *The Newberry News*. The late Richard C. Hulbert, Pensacola, Florida, provided much-needed information on the pine lumbering era. His painstaking cooperation in response to my many inquiries was invaluable. As Nick Eggenhofer made his illustrations for this work, he provided the equivalent of highly skilled collaboration, capturing the moods of the North far better than I could hope to do with words. To my son Charlie I am grateful for his conscientious photographic work, both with the camera and in the darkroom, enlarging and preserving rare old photographs.

Many other persons have befriended me at intervals in this searching. I wish to acknowledge these kindnesses gratefully. Not a few who came to my aid have died in the past decade or so, and it is with the regret that must accompany so belated a thanks that I include some of their names here, among those of others who have been especially helpful: James M. Babcock, Jesse Barrett, Condon Bartlett, R.J. Beach, Kenyon Boyer, John Cameron, Dr. E.H. Campbell, Mrs. Mary Chamberlain, William J. Chesbrough, Alice Clapp, William H. Clarke, John Cumming, Sidney D. Foster, Merle B. Fretz, F.P. Furlong, Russell Goodeman, Dr. E.F. Greenman, Philip Hamilton, Mrs. Jennie House, John C. Hunter, Robert Hunter, Harriet Jameson, Geneva Kebler, Harold C. Lawrence, Jerry L. Lynch, Tom Marshall, Mrs. D.N. McLeod, Robert S. Moore, Dr. Grace Lee Nute, Olive Pendill, J.P. Rahilly, Phyllis Rankin, Will Ranson, Dr. L.E. Read, Eino Sainio, Ruth Schoonover, Matt Surrell and Renville Wheat.

Sprague Taylor, 1940.

To my father, Charles Taylor, my guide and mentor when I first entered the Tahquamenon woods, goes a final note of appreciation for many days spent together in the quiet company of its trees.

Sprague Taylor

River of Legend

It has been called Michigan's Wilderness River, and probably no other stream in the state is more nearly that. But the Tahquamenon is a river of contrasts, defying attempts at precise characterization. For a hundred miles, taking all its meanderings into account, it flows through plains and heavy timber, marshy flats and thickets. It is a river given to the woods, yet where the plow has made brief contact near its banks, the scene is almost pastoral. It is a river of silences, but thunder rides its murky depths. Like the varied landscape that lends it passage, the Tahquamenon turns many faces to the northern sky.

There is a corner in the southeast quadrant of this landscape that I came to know well as a youth. Small wonder to me then, when I riffle notes and sort remembrances for a beginning, that the place names of early years keep crowding up. They tell of haunts learned with gun and rod when I grew up in the village

of Hulbert beside one of the tributaries, the East Branch.
Inevitably they are forest names, seldom if ever written down.
Hardwood Island, for instance, near which in early fall the bucks
rubbed velvet from their antlers on the speckled alder; or Big
Bayou - where there were trout we called "the old raunchers"
- and always, it seemed, the sound of white-throat, joyously alive
on a distant dead tamarack, or of bittern, chunk-a-lunking a weird
signal amid the marsh grass and cattails. Glacial trickery had given
us Devil's Pocket; not far away, and good for dry walking, was
Horseshoe Ridge. Unless, of course, we were headed home by
way of Corduroy Road. Looming large among all such names was
the one given the Tahquamenon, as when someone might
volunteer, "I hear they're bitin' down on the Mainstream."

The Mainstream, yes. Surely that had a fine, direct
appropriateness. None of our other rivers had spread the channel
of its influence so deeply into our lives. Yet none was so remote,
or so darkly secret in its coursing. When, in time, one will turn
from the horizon of memory of such a place, and seek to learn
more about it in whatever ways he knows, it has seemed to me
that one will finally discover a youthful wonder about it still
there, still pulling, despite all the yield of diaries and interviews
and fragile maps. And it will remain there at work, an indefinable
spell, in whatever one calls to mind about the country of youth,
or the people of home.

Searching for the derivation of the name of the river, humans
have supplied many versions of their own. River of Head Winds,
they have said, maintaining that they bucked the wind on its
lower reaches no matter what the direction of paddling. Others,
mindful of its windings, have called it River of a Hundred Bends.
Twentieth-century descendants of the local Chippewa Indians
have differed, and puzzling over it, have come up with
translations ranging from "river up against a hill" and "lost
woman river" to "river with the island part way." The original
meaning appears - as the scholarly Jesuit, Father William
Gagnieur, concluded in 1930 - "to be lost in the long past."

The origin of the present spelling is easier to trace. On the
remarkable Jesuit map of Lake Superior published in 1672 the
small island lying five miles off the mouth of the river in what
is now known as Whitefish Bay is called "Outa koua minan."
"Outaouaks" was a term applied by the French to some bands
of natives met in their earliest encounters in the Great Lakes

region. There are reasons to believe that "Outa koua minan" was intended to refer to the berry fields of these natives.

Whatever the original meaning, missionaries and treaty makers tackled the spelling of the name phonetically and arrived at an array of tongue-twisters: Otahquamenaw, Otikwaminag, Tacquimenon and Tackwymenon, among others. Longfellow adopted Taquamenaw in his *Song of Hiawatha*, and to make it fit his meter, pronounced it Taqua*me*naw.

The main river rises in a series of glacial pit lakes and ponds at the western boundary of Luce County about fourteen miles south of Lake Superior. Approaching the headwaters from the south, one will find the stream little more than a brook, its current fairly swift as it glides between birch-clad banks. Here it is pine country, open and fire-scarred, though second growth flourishes along the river bottom. Occasionally there are hunting camps, occupied for a little while each year. The few roads are largely unimproved. Some owe their existence to old railroad grades; nearly all of them remain unplowed in winter.

As it enters the broad depression stretching east and west across the county, the Tahquamenon widens and its current slackens. A score of small feeders have swelled it, and the pools have begun to take on the brownish tinge imparted by miles of peat-bottomed swamp. Hill-born, it now begins its course across a wide, pre-glacial trough. On the southern border lie the settlements of McMillan and Dollarville, and not far downstream is Newberry, the principal town of the region. The traveler on Highway M-28 obtains a good view of this valley, especially from points on either side of McMillan. Northward stretches a spruce and tamarack lowland, its floor cushioned with sphagnum moss - almost as much a wilderness as when the natives gazed at it from their maple sugar camp on the hill west of the village.

Both above and below Newberry are "The Spreads" where the river overflows its banks during the spring freshet. Not far away is the clearing marking the site of Deadman's Farm. Shortly, after its largest tributaries - Sage, Hendrie and East Branch - have emptied into it, the river turns north. Now, with nearly a mile between some of the bends, the banks rise, the timber changes. In place of elm, ash and soft maple flats, the eye begins to encounter long vistas of white birch and hemlock. Behind these lie uplands clothed in the dignified greenery of hard maple, that tree prized by early natives and called, simply, "Sugar" in the notes of the first surveyors.

From here on, scattered white pines rear above the rest of the timber. If pine is indeed the mother of legend, it is here that at least one of her children was nurtured. For it was on these banks, wrote Longfellow, that Hiawatha fashioned his canoe; and downstream that his friend Kwasind, the strong man, cleared the river of the obstructions "to make a pathway for the people." The scene drawn in faraway Cambridge finds modest commemoration in Hiawatha Creek, a clear little run emptying just below the mouth of the East Branch.

This is the river of excursion boats, of hunters' cabins whose occupants, three or four hundred of them, invade the region every fall during the November deer season. Near one such camp are the remains of pilings that Con Culhane, the noted logger, drove down for his railroad bridge. Caught in a sweeping bight (a bend) a mile and a half downstream lies Big Island, the river's largest.

Soon the banks rise to levels of fifty feet or more, the channel narrows slightly; and after a burning on the west bank is passed, the current quickens. Less than a mile distant rises the muffled thunder of one of the Midwest's natural wonders, the Upper Falls.

Descriptions of this waterfall have ranged from the rather detached reports of such famous early visitors as Henry

Sprague Taylor

The Upper Falls in winter.

Sprague Taylor

A scene at the Lower Falls.

Schoolcraft and Douglass Houghton, to paeans of praise in distant newspapers. It attracts hundreds of thousands of visitors annually. For many of them it furnishes a spectacle to be watched on recurring trips, and by the hour.

Breaking through the height that crosses part of Tahquamenon country, the river takes a sheer plunge of nearly fifty feet over a ledge of Cambrian sandstone. On either side are steep, timbered banks; below is a winding gorge.

In the spring flood a torrent churns at the base of the drop with a full-throated roar; during summer the volume lessens, making the fall one of entrancing loveliness, a study in white and amber, set against the varied greens of the forest. But if the scene is captivating in these seasons, and superb when viewed against the multi-colored foliage of early October, on a bright morning in February or March it is dazzling. By then the backdrop has changed from green, combined with the delicate colors of sandstone walls at either side, to a gleaming array of stalactitic ice formations, shining in pale shades of green, blue and yellow. Above, coated with a feathery spray, the birches on the southern height are outlined starkly against the sky. The sun looks full upon the brink, making rainbows of the rising mist.

With the Lower Falls, four miles beyond, the descent to an

elevation of only four feet above Lake Superior is completed. Between the crest of the Upper Falls and quiet reaches just below the Lower Falls there is a total drop of eighty-eight feet. At the Lower Falls, where two drops in the main waterfall account for twenty feet of the descent, the thunder is muted. The channel divides to form a rock-bound, wooded island around which the river plunges in a series of cataracts, the favorites of some who compare them with the single fall upstream. Though they lack the majesty of the Upper Falls, their short leaps lend an accent of airy grace to the beauty of the surroundings.

By this time the traveler has entered Chippewa County. Northward are the hills that bend the channel east toward Whitefish Bay. The watercourse has narrowed; small spring creeks are to be the only tributaries for the last fifteen miles, part of it through hardwoods, part of it through pine country.

Nearly all of the big pines are gone now, and the rollways from which the logs were tumbled into the water are growing thick with young trees. Aloof and quiet, its breadth increased in places to nearly a hundred yards, the river moves past the ruins of logging camps and trappers' cabins. Its silence is seldom broken, and then chiefly by the motors of a few summer fishermen or fall hunters, together with those sounds that were the same when dynasties of great pines were seedlings: the chatter of a kingfisher, swooping in the halflight of daybreak for his breakfast; the guttural colloquy of northern ravens; the "thwack!" of a beaver's tail on a still evening; and in the expectant quiet of a winter night, the howls of a stray timber wolf.

Seen in terms of geologic time, much of Tahquamenon surface topography is young. Some seven or eight thousand years have passed, it is estimated, since glacial ice last retreated northward and left behind its distinctive features - deep-walled lakes and the high moraine forming the south rim of a main section of the river valley.

During one stage in the development of the drainage system, a gradual uplift is believed to have raised the ledge at the Upper Falls. This reduced the current and accounted partly for the accumulation of peat and muck that is the Great Tahquamenon Swamp.

Actually it is a series of connected swamps, each belonging to its own tributary. Thus the East Branch Swamp, stretching eastward past the villages of Hulbert, Eckerman and Strongs; the

Hendrie and Sage Swamps, thrusting southward to high plateaus marking the watershed dividing Lake Superior and Lake Michigan streams; and Murphy Swamp, a belt of lowland bordering the main river on its northward course. Once you leave the few settlements behind, you will find these areas to be almost uninhabited. On many a mile-square section a man-track is as rare as a boulder. Ridges formed of sand by ancient combinations of wind and water action dot the entire lowland, reminders that in what geologists call Lake Algonquin time, this swampland lay largely submerged. Numerous creeks furnish good, if sometimes strenuous, fishing. Long gone are the passenger pigeons, not so long the fisher and pine marten; but deer yard in winter coverts in large numbers, and bears still hibernate beneath upturned roots and jampiles. Hunter and hunted continue to enact the age-old rituals of the chase. Tahquamenon country, above all, is wildlife country.

Historically it is old, though the adventurous who entered Lake Superior in the seventeenth and eighteenth centuries were content largely to pass it by, and to press on to the greater promise beckoning far to the west and north of the lake. Turning a glance into its past, one may miss the ring of famous names or the stir of great events. But since history is also made of quieter stuff, it may be that these parts of the story will bear telling in its name.

As they made the long traverse across the bay to round Whitefish Point - or "la pointe aux poissons blancs," as the early French knew it - voyageurs singing their *chansons*, and black-robed Jesuits bound for distant missions, might take refuge at the mouth of the river or beach their canoes at the small island, five miles offshore. "I set out the next day [from the Sault] and slept at the riviere tak-quiminan," says Jean Baptiste Perreault, a trader on the upper Mississippi, in an account of the travels he undertook in 1791. His entry is typical of the scanty references to the river before 1800.

The obscurity cloaking the watercourse for nearly two centuries may be ascribed partly to the fact that Sault Ste. Marie, strategically located at the outlet of Lake Superior forty miles to the east, was to play a dominant role in the history of the lake from the very first. There Tahquamenon natives made contact with the Jesuits; there on June 14, 1671, they witnessed the ceremony by which the representative of Louis XIV took possession for France of Lake Superior and areas "adjacent thereto, those discovered and to be discovered." At the Sault also, through the long period marking the reign of fur in the north country, the natives found men eager to barter for the results of the winter hunt.

But the fur traders, in turn, came to know the Tahquamenon. We have this about it from John Johnston, a leading figure at the Sault in the first quarter of the 1800's: "There are many advantages which should induce farmers to settle here; the soil is excellent, very little underwood and large improvable meadows. There is a fall about three leagues up the river where in spring you may take any quantity of sturgeon."

When Johnston wrote - somewhat optimistically - about the prospects for settlers in 1807, more than a hundred and fifty years had elapsed since the Jesuits first saw the curve at the mouth of the river. In that time this region of eight hundred square miles lay almost dormant. Its day would come. Meanwhile the portage paths around the falls were being worn smooth by moccasined feet. The "thunder-harp" of the pines lifted new strings to the wind, and at intervals, the fires of lonely bivouacs gleamed along the wide arm of Whitefish Bay.

Shingabawossin's People

When the celebrated Dr. Douglass Houghton, Michigan's first state geologist, canoed up the Tahquamenon as far as the Upper Falls in June 1840, he was quick to notice signs of native life along the river. Several families were engaged in fishing near the mouth. Just below the Lower Falls his party breakfasted at a clearing of "some 15 to 20 acres" which bore evidence of an earlier planting, and the path around the falls was well defined. "The route ... " Houghton made note, "bears evidence of being frequently traversed ... for the portage path is deeply worn and there are remains of Indian lodges at both ends ... The Indians residing upon the banks of the Tequoimenon formerly numbered vastly more than at the present day." Tribal traditions appear to corroborate this last statement.

These were the Canoe Indians of the North, of the tribe called Ojibwa, or more commonly now, Chippewa. Well-known in all

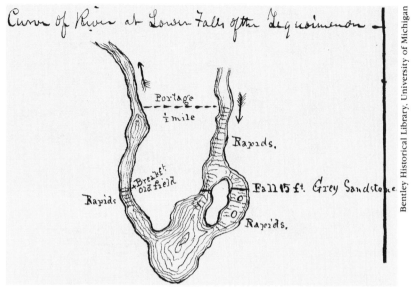

Curve of River at Lower Falls of the Tahquamenon

Portage
½ mile

Rapids.

Breakf't
old field

Rapids

Rapids

Fall 15 ft. Grey Sandstone

Rapids.

Douglass Houghton's 1840 sketch of the Lower Falls.

Lake Superior environs, it is a name strongly linked to the river. Their totemic emblem, the crane, belonged to the tribal division - called the clan - having orators who were acknowledged leaders in council. The Cranes, in addition, claimed some chieftainship over neighboring clans.

By 1650 they were known to the Jesuits; how long before they had roamed the Tahquamenon country in their westward movement is not known. It has been set down at a generation or two, perhaps more. At times in that dawning of the lake's recorded history they were called Saulteurs, or the nation of the Sault. Their hereditary enemies were chiefly the Iroquois, Sioux and Fox. A still- cherished tradition fixes the bloody repulse of the Iroquois in the mid-1600's at a point bearing the name of that tribe on the southern shore of Whitefish Bay. Intermittent struggles with the Sioux continued until well into the nineteenth century.

Here these people of the Crane clan eked out a precarious existence. Northward loomed the Big Lake, the Gitche Gumee of fabled lore; southward, Ottawa, Potawatomi, and Menomini tribes held sway in a more hospitable climate. The Tahquamenon Chippewa ranged between.

Other native cultures had existed here in the gloom of prehistory. Sifting the finds from their obscure tenancies, archaeologists set them apart in time with terms loosely categorical, such as Boreal Archaic, or Old Copper, or Early Woodland. With new techniques (radiocarbon dating is an example), much more can be learned about human occupancy of the region. But the unraveling of this skein of the past will take long. Meanwhile some evidence accidentally turns up. Of that kind is this quartzlike blade, lying here on the desk beside me. It was found by a trapper in a freshly bulldozed road near Hulbert in 1956. To attempt to glance back to the time of its fashioning is to try to span not years, but centuries, and perhaps fifty of them, at that.

Archaeological explorations in 1966 and 1967 at Naomikong Point in lower Whitefish Bay have proven it to be one of the most significant sites in the upper Great Lakes of the Middle Woodland culture (between 200 B.C. and A.D. 800). The location (more specifically, west of Menekaunee Point) had been known for years as a place of native encampment, but its potential for the revelation of prehistoric habitation apparently had not been recognized.

On a snowy day in October 1964, at my invitation, George I. Quimby, a nationally known authority on archaeology, accompanied me to Naomikong Point. Author of *Indian Life in the Upper Great Lakes*, he was at that time with the Chicago Natural History Museum. From his observations at the site, coupled with his examination of the many artifacts that my son and I had found awash on the beach there, he concurred in our belief that this area, protected as it is from the sweep of Superior's northwesters, would prove to be a finding place of major importance on the Upper Peninsula's northern border.

Quimby relayed information about his initial visit to Naomikong to Dr. James E. Fitting at the Museum of Anthropology, University of Michigan. On June 19, 1965, they conducted a joint archaeological survey. Wearing wet-suits and scuba gear, three divers searched a section of the lake which had been laid out in a grid, and recovered 264 fragments of pottery, plus other artifacts. By August, the Museum of Anthropology had received from the United States Forest Service permission to excavate on the site. The summer of 1966 found a team of college students working there under Fitting's direction. They went about the project in the most methodical fashion, mapping,

James Fitting

Charles G. Taylor at work at a "dig."

photographing, testing, and sampling as they uncovered the ground and went down; and they recovered an immense number of potsherds.

In July and August of 1967 the "dig" went on, directed by Donald E. Janzen, who had assisted on the previous work. A total of 2,750 square feet was excavated in the two seasons. In the collection analyzed, catalogued, and stored at the museum were over 133,000 shards of pottery, 1,882 flint scrapers, 49 projectile points, and a smaller number of stone and copper tools. Janzen's 1968 doctoral dissertation, *The Naomikong Point Site and the Dimensions of Laurel in the Lake Superior Region*, describes in detail the archaeological material found. Although some artifacts from the Late Woodland period (roughly, A.D. 800 to A.D. 1600) were recovered, the great majority were of Middle Woodland origin, prior to A.D. 450. They were attributed by Janzen to the Laurel culture, which was first identified in excavations in northern Minnesota between 1933 and 1940. Several other Laurel sites have been discovered since then, all adjacent to either lakes or rivers, suggesting that they may have been good locations for fishing. The chief defining characteristic is a similarity in pottery types. Janzen has written:

Laurel, originally defined by Wilford (1941) for a Middle Woodland manifestation in northern Minnesota, has now been extended to include parts of the provinces of Ontario, Manitoba, and Saskatchewan. Recently Mason (1967) called attention to a Laurel-like component of the Door Peninsula in Wisconsin, thus initiating this area into the Laurel family. Prior to work at Naomikong Point, the spatial distribution of Laurel sites excluded the south shore of Lake Superior, and this region was considered marginal to the major

C.G. Taylor

Tahquamenon Country prehistoric artifacts

development whose focal point was to the north and west. The Naomikong Point site has not only yielded Laurel ceramics, but has done so in a quantity so far unmatched at any other site. One of its contributions has been to extend the southern limits of Laurel and thereby demonstrate a far greater range to this culture than once imagined.

Pottery fragments, grit-tempered and variously decorated, still shift in the eroding wash of Whitefish Bay. With them mingle the plain leavings of later trade: French clay pipe, English gunflint, pieces of American crockery. And nearby, indestructibly evocative, sleep the arrowheads, in Thoreau's happy phrase, "in the skin of the revolving earth."

Through ice-free months the local Chippewa sought out favorite fishing sites - the main river below the Lower Falls for sturgeon, Whitefish Point, Naomikong Point or the St. Marys at Sault Ste. Marie for whitefish. *Poisson blanc bouillon*, as the French called whitefish delicately boiled high over a small fire, was a staple food. Setting up the oval bark lodges, which one writer likened to upside-down birds' nests, they might remain in one place long enough to plant small fields of "mondamin," their corn. Later, in the 1840's of Houghton's time, their chief crop was potatoes; but even then, as government census takers

C.G. Taylor

Rim fragments of Woodland Period pottery from Whitefish Bay.

were apt to put it, they were largely "subsisting by the chase." These were the months for the building of birch-bark canoes. Equipped with simple tools, they worked with cedar ribs, pieces of bark, gum and the split root threads known as "wattap" to fashion a craft of singular usefulness. To poet William Cullen Bryant, who inspected examples at the Sault in 1846, it was "one of the most beautiful and perfect things of the kind constructed by human art."

Before frosts spelled the approach of the winter hunt, the Chippewa woman, heavily laden with her foraging, left her toed-in tracks on the portages. There were roots to gather for remedies, blueberries to pick on burned-over plains, and cranberries to be had from such favorite bogs as the one at the east end of Betsy Lake. Rolls of bark from both birch and cedar were saved for lodge building and repair; mats for the interiors were woven from rushes. Occasionally, the tasks of her simple housekeeping done, a mother hung her youngest child in its carved cradle, the "tikanogun," from the limb of a nearby tree and worked with beads or dyed porcupine quills. Ravages of smallpox, cholera, scarlet fever and erysipelas periodically swept through the lodges; infant mortality was high.

Nomadic by necessity, they were often on their ancient trails. A main pathway led from the foot of Whitefish Bay southwesterly

C.G. Taylor

Trade axe and hoe from Sec. 10, 47-6 near Whitefish Point.

to the Tahquamenon near the mouth of the Hendrie, and in their trips into the interior it was often used as a short-cut. Between the west end of Hulbert Lake and the north side of Big Carp Lake there was a trail that could still be detected in stretches in the 1920's. Another ran west from the Lower Falls village site to Grand Marais, cutting off the long, roundabout lakeshore route by way of Whitefish Point. Before the establishment of railroad communication in the 1880's, Indian mail carriers, urging on their dogs ahead of light toboggans, sometimes followed it as part of the winter route between the Sault and Marquette. Still other trails connected the river with the Manistique Lakes.

Frequently the Tahquamenon Chippewa paid prolonged visits to the trading and fishing centers at the Sault or on the principal nearby islands - Grand, Drummond, Manitoulin or Mackinac. International boundary lines meant little; they moved back and forth across the St. Marys River to British Canada freely.

When, his meager outfitting completed, the hunter returned

with his family to his wintering ground, it was in the timeless pursuit of meat and fur. Before trade traps and guns came into his hands, he relied upon snares, deadfalls, his bow and spear, and above all, upon an animal-like stealth and cunning. During deep snows he might hunt unsuccessfully for days. He worked from the old encampments he knew by such names as Wapukwakag, Wequetong, Monuaweanin or Kashingwakuka-gomag, and beside small creeks known to us now as Teaspoon, Gimlet or Roxbury. There he sought colonies of beaver, those busy rodents for whose skins financiers staked livres, pounds and hard Yankee dollars in that episodic, far-flung commerce of the North.

He took mink, otter and muskrat also on the watercourses; wolves and foxes, together with their natural prey, deer and rabbits, in swamp coverts; along pine ridges, their favorite haunts, he tried for marten. If the hunt went well the heavy odor of beaver skins, drying on a hooplike frame, or of muskrat carcasses, freshly peeled, filled the dim, smoky interior of the lodge. Without game the hunter puffed stoically on his pipe, or recited all the day's dire omens that had augured ill for him.

If he lacked the political organization of such tribes as the Iroquois, he had his own secret medicine society, the "midewiwin." He lived in a world of dreams and spirits, and around them he fashioned his mythology. Behind the face of a watch a spirit was at work; in the phenomenon of fire he glimpsed another. As the northern lights streaked the night sky, he saw the shades of his ancestors wandering; and now that it was winter, when he reasoned that all the beings who peopled his thoughts were asleep, he recounted their exploits. Out of tales dating from the age of flint and pottery the fabled names echoed once more: Gitche Manito and Matche Manito, good and evil respectively; Manabozho, the fabulous god; Kwasind, the strong man; Shawondasee, the South Wind, and his three brothers; and a host of others.

Beneath one of the cataracts at the Lower Falls, one story ran, lived a spirit whose sorcery was responsible for the appearance of giant sturgeon with human heads. Woe to the fisherman who speared or hooked one of them, for he inevitably vanished, to reappear the following year in its form. Once in the Tahquamenon in large numbers, this great fish, the "nahma," figured importantly in their legends. One bend about six miles above the mouth of the river they named Nahmawashing, or Sturgeon Den, from a belief that the sturgeon found at the Lower Falls in the spring came through an underground channel connecting this deep hole with Whitefish Bay. There were lurid accounts of lone spearers who ventured out at night with their torches, never to be seen again; and from old Agindosh ("One Who Counts") came a tale of metamorphosis involving the change of drowned hunters to pike at his wintering ground on Sheephead Lake.

If he tired of manitos or windigos, the Tahquamenon storyteller could turn to the feats of his ancestors. He might tell about Mackobwam (a variant of Muckwa-boam, "Bear's Thigh"), a famed runner, and about how he could make the overland trip between Naomikong Point and the site of Munising, at least eighty miles, within the hours of daylight. Or how, as an old man, he beat a champion Cree from Canada in a grueling race from the mouth of the river to Whitefish Point and back.

For a tale with melodramatic overtones there was a legend built around the Upper Falls. During an ancient foray near the mouth of the river, it was told, some Menomini warriors captured a small Chippewa girl. Years passed; she became a beautiful young woman. When the Menomini again sent a war party against her people, they were sure of her loyalty and depended upon her to guide them. From Lake Michigan they paddled up the Manistique and the Fox to the portage forming the connection with the Tahquamenon. Realizing that these warriors, unlike her captors, were unfamiliar with the river, she resorted to a desperate stratagem. While they paddled downstream near the Upper Falls, she burst into song. The heavily laden canoes gathered momentum in the rapids as the entire party joined in a wild chant. When they heard the ominous rumble it was too late. All were swept to their deaths over the brink. "In this manner," one version concludes, "did the beautiful Ojibwa maiden save her own people and avenge her wrongs." The imagery of Tahquamenon native people spread its deepest roots in the winter lodge.

Meanwhile, furs and deerskins were being bundled into packs to be applied against the credits in cloth, powder and lead, traps or kettles received the preceding fall. To trace the steps by which local peltry ultimately reached the fur capitals of Montreal, London or Leipzig would be to attempt a volume by itself. But from the roll of those who dealt in it - chiefly from the Sault or Mackinac Island - a few names may be called. There was Alexander Henry, the adventurous Englishman whose account of his varied fortunes, including his escape from the massacre at Fort Michilimackinac in 1763, has much in it to intrigue the reader. His one-time partner, Jean Baptiste Cadotte, was a leading figure in the trade of that period. Succeeding Cadotte at the Sault was John Johnston, whose story is told in detail in Janet Lewis' novel, *The Invasion*.

Who will doubt that Tahquamenon furs were involved in 1818, as Ramsay Crooks sat down at his Mackinac Island headquarters and wrote to John Jacob Astor, head of the sprawling American Fur Company, asking that Johnston's packs be reserved for sale in London because the Sault trader felt he obtained better prices there? Nearly twenty years later Gabriel Franchere, the firm's factor (agent) at the Sault, was writing, "From what I can learn from the Indians of Taquaminan this will be a good Marten hunting season." Early in the summer of 1837 Peter Barbeau was busy picking up furs and maple sugar with the company scow. In the mid-1860's, long after the American Fur Company had failed, he would be buying on his own. Earlier, about 1832, when a government census report placed the population of the local natives at 186, traders William Johnston, Edward Cadotte and Eustache Raussain were licensed to deal for furs at "Tacquimenon." At the same time, William Johnston held a license to fish at Whitefish Point.

The value of his furs to the Tahquamenon hunter of 1831 is revealed in a report of the Indian Agent for the region, Henry Rowe Schoolcraft:

At this post (St. Maries) the rate of barter may be stated thus. For a 3 pt Blanket two plus [the value of a prime beaver skin]. For a N.W. gun 4 plus. For a beaver trap two plus. For a fathom of Strouds [a kind of blanket cloth, manufactured especially for Indian trade] 2 plus, for a fathom of Superfine cloth 3 or 4 plus. For a bag of flour 2 plus. In adjusting the acct a bear, an otter skin or a beaver of the third year, are counted respectively two plus. Ten muskrats or 3 martins, one plus.

Late in March, the Chippewa's crust-moon, winter camps were

generally abandoned in favor of groves of hard maple. In what was perhaps the happiest time of the year, families flocked to the present location of Newberry, to points on the south bank of the river below the Lower Falls and, principally, to bluffs overlooking the southern shore of the bay. Tapping trees and collecting the sweet sap, boiling it down to different consistencies, filling birch-bark containers, the "makoks," with the brown, nourishing sugar - these were the tasks of a festive month. What "springing out" was to the Tahquamenon lumberjack much later, sugar-making time was to his predecessor.

So the fortunes of the Chippewa were caught up in a seasonal ebb and change. Henry Rowe Schoolcraft was moved to pay them tribute. "No people," he wrote, "are more easy, or less clamorous under sufferings of the deepest dye, and none more happy, or more prone to evince their happiness, when prosperous in their affairs." As Indian Agent for the federal government - at the Sault from 1822 to 1833 and then at Mackinac Island until 1841 - Schoolcraft was often in touch with members of the Tahquamenon band.

Anticipating the modern tourist by more than a hundred years, he made a trip up the river early in the summer of 1824, accompanied by Chippewa canoemen and an interpreter.

On the second day [he has written], we reached and entered the Tacquimenon River. It carried a deep and strong current to the foot of the first falls, which they call Fairy Rocks. This Indian word denotes a species of little men or fairies, which, they say, love to dwell on rocks....

He refers to the "peculiarly sylvan air" of the Lower Falls, and finds the rapids above them a perfect torrent.

... but before I was well aware of it, they had the canoe in it, with a single man with a long pole in the bow and stern. I took my seat between the centre bars, and was in admiration at the perfect composure and "sang froid" with which these two men managed it - now shooting across the stream to find better water, and always putting in their poles exactly at the right instant, and singing some Indian cantata all the while. The upper falls at length burst on our view.... The water forms a complete curtain.... They said there was some danger of the canoe's being drawn under the sheet, by a kind of suction.

Impressed by the unexpected cordiality of his companions, he concludes:

> I threw myself, naked handed, into their midst, and was received with a noble spirit of hospitality and welcome. And the incidents of this trip revealed to me some of the most interesting scenes of Indian domestic life.

All who are attracted to Tahquamenon lore will remain in Schoolcraft's debt. The story of his marriage to the granddaughter of a noted Ojibwa chief, Waub-ojeeg, and his preparation of a monumental collection of Indian mythology, language and customs is becoming widely known. Upon the material in his volumes, Longfellow drew heavily for *The Song of Hiawatha*, first published in 1855. Generations of school children have chanted

> "And thus sailed my Hiawatha down the rushing Tahquamenaw... ."

By 1827 Schoolcraft had included in *The Literary Voyageur* - one of the manuscript periodicals he circulated at intervals - a legend titled "Origin of the Miscodeed [the spring beauty, a northern wildflower], or the Maid of Taquimenan." Dr. Philip P. Mason, Schoolcraft authority and editor, in his 1962 compilation of material from surviving issues of the magazine, explained that this contribution was the work of Schoolcraft's wife Jane. It is an interesting example of a literary approach of the period. It tells of an attack on a Tahquamenon Chippewa family by a "daring war party of the treacherous Mendawakantons [belonging to the Dakota Sioux] from the Mississippi." The tone is shown in the conclusion:

> With loud yells and rapid footsteps the foe entered. Conspicuous, in front, stood the eldest son of a warrior who had been killed by the Chippewas in the great battle of the falls of the river St. Croix. His brows were painted red, and his spear poised. But the work of death was soon finished.

*Origin of the Miscodeed.**
or the
Maid of Taquimenon.

The daughter of Mongazida, was the pride of her parents, and their only child. Beauty sat upon her lips, and life and animation marked all her motions. Fourteen summers had witnessed the growth of her stature, and the unfolding of her charms, and each spring, as it came around, had beheld her, in her happy simplicity, revelling amid the wild flowers of her native valley. There was no valley so sweet as the valley of Taquimenon. There, she listened to the earliest notes of the wild birds, who returned from the south, to enliven the forests after the repose of winter; and there, also, she had prepared

* *Claytonia Virginica.*

Specimen page from Schoolcraft's *Tahquamenon Legend*

There lay, motionless, the husband and the wife alike beyond the influence of hope or fear, hate or harm. But no other human form appeared, and the eye of the savage leader rolled in disappointment around, as he viewed the spot where Miscodeed, his meditated victim, had sunk into the earth. A small and beautiful white bird was seen to fly from the top of the lodge. It was the guardian spirit of Miscodeed. The knife and the tomahawk were cheated of their prey - her guardian angel had saved her from being the slave of her enemy.... When the friends of the slaughtered family visited the silent lodge ... all they saw on the ground where the maid of Taquimenon had fallen, was a modest little white flower, bordered with pink, which was at once supposed to be her emblem.

A stopover at Whitefish Point early in September 1835 is described by Chandler Robbins Gilman in his journal, published the next year under the title *Life on the Lakes, Being Tales & Sketches Collected During a Trip to the Pictured Rocks of Lake Superior.* With a friend he had come by steamer from New York to Mackinac Island. There he visited with Schoolcraft, whose studies of native culture he had read. He secured a canoe from the American Fur Company and hired a crew, including as a guide Charles Cloutier, "an old half-breed," he wrote, "who has been five and thirty years a 'voyageur' on the lake."

Of the approach to the mouth of the "Tequamenon," Gilman recorded:

The water of this river is of a deep ruby tint ... and when viewed in the stream it looks nearly as dark as port wine. The colour, I believe, is communicated by the decaying vegetable matter in the marshes through which it passes....

Here we landed and found the frames of several Indian lodges, near one of them a canoe.... Wandering a little way back from the lodges, we found an Indian grave. It was inclosed by a wall of logs two feet high, and carpeted with birch bark; a steep cedar roof completed what might be literally called the narrow house. Cloutier said it was the grave of a chief who ruled over the division of Chippewas inhabiting this part of the lake and holding their council fire here; his name "Mukwa-boam."

Having left "hieroglyphics" on the canoe for its absent owner, and pilfered the skin of a "little Carriboo" from the grave site, the travelers rowed on up the shore, noting the mouth of the Shelldrake, and once again the "ruby coloured water." Upon arrival at Whitefish Point:

... a white man ... made his appearance, and hailed us in

McKenney & Hall, *History of the Indian Tribes of North America*

Two portraits of Chief Shingabawossin, based on sketches by J.O. Lewis in 1826 at Fond du Lac.

a very friendly manner, though the noise of the surf rendered his words inaudible. He pointed out, however, the best place to land; and when we got ashore, greeted Cloutier as an old friend, and invited us very cordially to his cabin, assuring us ... that proceeding further was totally out of the question in the present state of the weather. He was soon joined by a dozen Indians and half-breeds - men, women, and children... . There is now a regular fishing establishment, and all these people are dependent upon it.

... we made our way to the first hut.... The cabin, perhaps twenty feet square, without floor ... is lined inside with strips of birch bark, bits of old matting, and part of a tattered blanket; the roof is, as usual, of cedar bark, with a hole in the centre to give egress to some part of the smoke from a fire in the middle ... which, chilled and wet as we were, was most welcome.

With a gift of whitefish from their host "to raise comfort to happiness," the group ate, explored the Point, "a very good place to collect mineralogical specimens," visited with the residents, and slept that night crowded into the little hut. At sunrise on September 11, they were on their way in good weather to Grand Marais, observing the shore along the route. Of the entrance of the "Two Heart" or "Twin" Gilman noted " ... it is a sweet spot, and the traditions of the Indians have made it the retreat of two devoted lovers, who 'the world forgetting and by the world forgot,' made their happy home in this secluded valley."

Shingabawossin, as his name is most often written now, meaning "Image Stone," was the most important figure among natives associated with the Tahquamenon after 1800. Of an old ruling family, he was to be recognized as the leading chief of the Upper Peninsula before his death in 1828. "A tall, majestic, and graceful person," according to Schoolcraft, a warrior in youth and counselor of peace in old age, the influence he exerted was impressive.

By 1820 he and his followers faced the inevitability of occupation of their tribal domain. That year, at the Sault, the first in a series of treaties was signed. By its terms the natives of the vicinity ceded sixteen square miles - but not until after Shingabawossin had helped to persuade them to resume a broken negotiation.

No less than seven times were Tahquamenon chiefs to have their names affixed to treaties between 1820 and 1855. On three occasions Shingabawossin himself traveled long distances to take part in these councils. To Prairie du Chien, near the mouth of the Wisconsin, he went in 1825. The following year he was at Fond du Lac, at the head of Lake Superior; and a year later at Buttes des Mortes on the Fox River, a tributary of the Wisconsin. At Fond du Lac the government, aware of the presence of copper in Chippewa territory, put the question of mineral cession to the assemblage. Here again was Shingabawossin's prestige in evidence. No author of conspiracy or uprising, he was never destined to be as feared or lamented as Pontiac or Tecumseh or Black Hawk. His advice to young warriors was now framed simply: "Live in peace and follow the chase." True, he was said to have fought with distinction in the bloody skirmish with the Fox on the St. Croix River, but that was long before; inter-tribal strife was passing. He had conferred with Tecumseh. He had mourned the loss of a brother who joined the British standard and died with the great Shawnee at the Thames in the War of

1812. But even as his forebears had witnessed French control and its overthrow, so he had watched the ascendancy and downfall of the British. Did an uneasy discernment tell him now that those who spoke of a Great White Father in Washington had come to stay?

Gravely the old chief rose from his place among the delegates at Fond du Lac. If his sight was beginning to fail, his bearing was as erect as ever. A blue coat of military type had replaced the usual blanket; around his hair was a band of scarlet, above his collar a black neckcloth. While he spoke there was an attentive silence. "If you have copper on your lands," he said at last, "I advise you to sell it. It is of no use to us."

And so it was done. Shingabawossin's mark joined others on the document, and he returned home. If, in a bleak sequel, the Senate failed in its ratification of the treaty to approve certain provisions helpful to local natives - provisions that the chief had urged - there was little enough time given to him for resentment. In less than three years he was dead. The long annals he had helped to write were yet to close.

James Goeldi

"Saw some scenes like this up around the Two Hearted River some years ago." (James Goeldi)

Cabins on the Bay

The shore of Tahquamenaw Bay, as all of Lake Superior's Whitefish Bay was often called in the nineteenth century, still retained much of its ancient solitude in the 1830's. Far to the south a tide of settlement moved east to west across Michigan Territory, but it would take nearly fifty years to reach the river. When settlement finally came, attracted more by timber than by land, the covered wagon and parchment window of pioneer lore lingered only in the tales of old men. During three decades preceding the Civil War, however, the narrow trails of history made by the natives gradually broadened under the tread of other feet.

After the death of Shingabawossin a dispute arose over the succession of the chieftainship. He had been one of nine brothers, several of whom acted as leaders of small groups of families. One of them, Kawgayosh ("Bird in Everlasting Flight"), finally chose

George Catlin

Chief Kawgayosh in 1836

to live on the Canadian side of the St. Marys River. He had known status as an orator and medicine man of some distinction, and his likeness survives today in a simple sketch drawn from life by America's much-traveled, sympathetic "Audubon of the Indians," George Catlin.

"This venerable chief," wrote Schoolcraft at Kawgayosh's death in 1836, "must have been about ninety. . . . His head was white. He was about six feet two inches in height, lithe of form, and long featured, with a grave countenance. . . . He was entitled to $500, under the treaty of 28th March, as one of the first class chiefs of his nation."

This treaty of March 28, 1836, was far-reaching in its consequence to the Chippewa and Ottawa of Michigan in that it provided for a cession to the United States of about sixteen million acres. It also established a reservation comprising most of the southern half of the Tahquamenon region with the river as its northern boundary. In the fall of that year members of the local band joined nearly 4,000 other natives at Mackinac Island to receive the first of their annuities - part in cash, part in goods. A list of the Tahquamenon band's apportionment of goods contains powder and shot, lead, flints, beaver traps, rice, saws, nails and putty. It also received - on a per capita basis - blankets ("one to each soul"), calico, sturgeon twine, brass kettles ("one to every three"), knives, axes, powder horns ("occasionally one"), and other articles. Coats and special powder horns were reserved for chiefs; their wives were given Prussian shawls.

By 1837 Shingabawossin's eldest son Kaybaynodin, or "Soft Wind," was acknowledged to be first chief. He presided over the dwindling destinies of his band until the Chippewa tribal organization was formally dissolved by the 1855 Treaty of Detroit. Missionaries of the period, regarding him with the deference due one of his waning authority, sometimes spoke of "the old chief" in their journals or reminiscences.

If only through their voluminous writings about an awakening frontier on Lake Superior, missionaries of the 1800's performed a valuable service to succeeding generations. Yet they were by no means simply Sunday exhorters or deskbound chroniclers. Here is the Reverend Abel Bingham, reporting a trip to the Tahquamenon band in January 1841: "I went up the Utikwamens river, or rather through the wilderness to

Rev. Abel Bingham

Wapukwagag which is one of their camping places on the river. In this tour I visited all of that band. Absent 11 days, preached 7 times."

The next year, after completing a 300-mile round trip along the south shore of Lake Superior by dog team, he writes in his journal: "Spent two days at Tequaminan, holding services as usual. Snow had fallen during our stay, making heavy traveling for the dogs. . . ." This entry concludes: "Was absent twenty-seven days, preached fourteen discourses, camped sixteen nights in the woods, and was detained one day by severe weather."

Abel Bingham stood at the forefront of a revival of religious activity that was to play a role in the development of Lake Superior during the second quarter of the 1800's. Preceding him and his contemporaries, both Catholic and Protestant, by more than a hundred years were the intrepid priests of the Society of Jesus. The names of Fathers Allouez, Marquette, Dreuillettes, Dablon and others will always lend an enduring interest to the larger story of the lake. But for a clearer picture of cross-cultural relationships in the Tahquamenon country, one must turn to a later period, and especially to men such as Abel Bingham.

A native of New Hampshire, a lieutenant severely wounded in the War of 1812, he had worked for about six years with the Seneca of New York. He moved to the Sault under Baptist auspices in 1828. While children of the Tahquamenon band were being enrolled in his boarding school, his letters to the Mission Board in Boston began to tell of visits to "the brethren at the Bay." Of all the outlying areas he reached, none was to be mentioned so frequently in his letters or journals of the next quarter-century (or to be treated with such a variation of spelling) as the one "embracing the Tikwamena country to Lake Michigan." By canoe or sailboat in summer, and by snowshoe and dogteam in winter, he made his rounds, laboring according to his lights and the doctrines of his times. With Shegud, whose name appears to defy translation, he formed a lasting friendship; the devoted Indian became a deacon in his church. Son-in-law of Shingabawossin, Shegud appears repeatedly in 1825-1850 writings about the river country.

Turning the pages of Bingham's journals, we will meet "Wamitigoshans, the Little Frenchman," at his winter camp near the mouth of Hendrie River, and sense his elation at having killed two deer with one shot; or Waysawedon ("Yellow Beard"), who "looked as if he had had a frolick, & just cooled off"; share a meal of fresh sturgeon at the mouth of the river with the widow of Shingabawossin, "the late great chief of the Utikwamena band"; learn of a boating tragedy that took the lives of "3 young men & a boy of our Tikuamina Indians"; visit with "Kah-ga-os [Kawgayosh], an old chief of the Te-qui-menon band"; listen to the chanting, "loud enough to stun a well person," of two medicine men at the foot of Tahquamenon Bay exhorting devils to leave the body of a sick tribesman; see the old chief, Kaybaynodin, who, in a devout repetition, "has renewed his pledge to abstain from drinking"; take the ailing Shegud on a ride in a cutter on the bay; travel upriver by dogteam "ten or fifteen miles" in three hours; hear of the latest doings of the enigmatic John Tanner, his interpreter in the 1830's, whose account of captivity has become a classic of Americana; help carry the litter of a young native near the Lower Falls who "was hunting ducks ... & his gun being out of order unexpectedly went off, & by some means the fire communicated with the powder in his horn hanging by his side, & blew him up"; and toward the end of his ministry find him admitting to his wife Hannah in 1852 that as he considers another trip to "Tikuamina," "I am satisfied that I can not stand either the fatigue, or the cold, as I have done in former years."

In writing of a stop at the Sault during his 1835 canoe trip to Lake Superior, diarist Gilman told of a visit with Bingham: "I had yesterday the pleasure of a long and very interesting interview with Mr. B[ingham], the Baptist Missionary at St. Marie; and his mild benevolent spirit, his gentle manners, and the resolute and patient firmness with which he devoted himself to his duty, had made a most agreeable impression on my mind."

According to Bingham's letters of 1829, members of the Tahquamenon band had begun to cultivate potatoes in clearings he had urged them to make about five miles south of the mouth of the river. Soon they were planting small crops of peas, beans and buckwheat in their enlarged fields, and he was encouraging them to form a permanent settlement around a mission school. The location of his school at the Sault had been criticized - by Schoolcraft, for one - who said it might serve more effectively if located "within the Indian country." On this subject Bingham wrote in the winter of 1843:

"I have been to Tikwamina & from thence one day's march into the wilderness where I visited Kebenodin, the principal chief of that band ... & other families.... As soon as he learned that we approved of Tikwamina ... he resolved to come down with me to present the subject in due form to their Agent."

As reasons for the Indian preference for the Tahquamenon location, he gives these:

"The hunting & fishing privileges there are superior to any other place on this side of the river [St. Marys]. 2nd. A number of families spend the whole winter there every year, & a considerable portion of the summer, spring, & fall...."

Before concluding this letter he adds his own recommendations:

"And among other privileges which the place affords, I may add that the wild meadows at the mouth of the river will afford an abundance of hay, sufficient for all the cattle that may be needed both for the mission & the Indians. The advantages for making sugar are also greater there than at any other place that has been examined."

The request for land was quickly denied by the Commissioner of Indian Affairs at Washington, who reminded Bingham that the natives lived near the Tahquamenon by sufferance only, and that they might be required to move at any time. (Kaybaynodin and his band had declined the government's offer of land west of the

Mississippi in 1838, and until 1841 were periodically disturbed by rumors that an exodus was still to take place.)

Undeterred, Bingham sought financial help from his mission board. Under the Treaty of 1836 the Indian Department was obliged to furnish a carpenter for the erection of houses, and the missionary now requested his services.

In October 1843 he wrote that he and the carpenter had been at the bay while a log house was put up for Shegud; in June 1845 he reported the building of four more. During the interval he had drawn up an agreement titled "Articles of Arrangement Between the Baptist Mission ... & the Ojibwa Indians at Takwamenong Relative to Forming a Settlement of the Indians at Tekwamena Bay," in order that the natives might obtain, among other benefits, "the habits of civilized life so far as the peculiarities of the country & climate will permit."

Next came the building of a rude home for his assistant. For this they carried boards, shingles and a team of oxen on the *Algonquin,* a small schooner then plying Lake Superior. Sailing deep into the bay, they anchored a mile offshore, made a raft of part of the lumber and with it landed the oxen. Logs had to be skidded from a cedar swamp over ground so soft that even this team, much better suited to the work than horses, could hardly manage it. The house up, Bingham reckoned its cost, aside from labor, at $236.98. It was the most pretentious dwelling in the entire region.

James Dougald Cameron, son of a prominent Hudson's Bay Company factor and a native woman of Canada's Nipigon country, was to live here for five or six years as "itinerating missionary." Shortly after meeting Bingham in 1832, he joined him as a helper. He spoke well in French, English or Chippewa, and he had been tutored in Greek and Latin. In the winter of 1834-35, at twenty-eight, he lived with members of the Tahquamenon band, and married Shingabawossin's youngest daughter. Two years later, again in the winter, he accompanied Shegud to the mouth of the river, where he found them under the influence of an old medicine man, "distinguished among them by the title of meta," and from there he went overland to Lake Michigan to visit one of the more distant bands. For more than twenty-five years his letters to the mission board at Boston were to tell of similar travels on both the north and south shores of Lake Superior.

Beneath the heading, "Tukwahminah Bay 22nd August 1847," he writes: "The young brethren are all occupied at Whitefish Point. They have salted upwards of eighty barrels of fish. Their crops look uncommonly well. During the winter they cut a goodly number of rails, and have this last spring enclosed their fields." The following spring he asks Bingham to provide them with "the following garden seeds, viz: one paper of onion ... one of cabbage, two of red beets ... one of Ruta Baga ... and also one paper of Water melon."

The nature of the change taking place in the 1840's is further shown by a census report made about the same time. During the year the band produced 1,500 bushels of potatoes and 6,000 pounds of maple sugar. Although 200 barrels of fish had been sold, only 200 skins are listed. The long years of living by the hunt were ending. As his share of the treaty payment, each person received - at the Sault now - a cash annuity of four dollars. The bounty of land and water was enough to prompt Bingham to write in 1848, "They made one haul early in the morning when I was at Tikuamina in which they brought in 6.5 Bbls. of Whitefish, & 11 sturgeon," and a year later to observe that the average amount of maple sugar produced by each family ranged from "5 to 600 or 700 pounds," and that the band had dug "a fine lot of potatoes." A cow and calf had been secured, and the sight of a mother feeding her children fresh milk and bread, in the missionary's view, "resembled more the habits of a New England farmer, than of an Indian of the forest."

For a while the settlement on the bay seemed destined to thrive. Then tragedy struck. In the winter of 1849 a wave of sickness, apparently erysipelas or cholera, swept through the cabins and lodges. Among other bereaved, Shegud buried his wife and daughter, Cameron his eldest son. Afterwards the place was never to be as fully occupied. Abandoning their old village site, some of the band came to prefer lodges near the site of the present Rivermouth Campground.

Meanwhile Abel Bingham continued his rounds, past sixty now, his tall frame leaner than ever, his wind-tanned face reflecting both benignity and sternness. Partly because the natives he served had dispersed - some of them moving to Canada - and partly because of the influence of other churches, he foresaw the closing of his Baptist School that was to occur in 1855. With wry humor he had written a dozen years before: "But while I labour,

& shake the bush, the Methodists watch & catch the bird . . . ."

Methodist activity culminated in the establishment of a mission at Naomikong in the fall of 1849. This shoal point, about six miles southeast of the mouth of the Tahquamenon, had long been a favorite fishery of the Chippewa. The Reverend John Pitezel, summing up his experiences later in his book *Lights and Shades of Missionary Life*, wrote that the site was selected "in a beautiful pine grove, on the shore of a little cove, or bay."

He could announce with pride a year later:

"At Naomikong we had purchased rising of sixty acres of land for the mission. The Indians had bought all around us, and were building considerably. We had built ... a comfortable schoolhouse, and made an addition to the mission house. Had also fitted up a comfortable dwelling for the interpreter."

Pitezel's report of 1851 listed as members of the church five whites and fifty-eight natives. Among the missionaries who lived at the shoal point were Peter Johnson, Salmon Steele and his brother Ebenezer, and Peter Marksman. Long after the mission had been abandoned (about 1853), Marksman remained a familiar figure between Whitefish Point, where his brother Wasquam (Lightning) had been a skilled fisherman, and the Sault. Like Cameron, he was part native. Like him, also, he turned to a lifetime of missionary work after meeting Bingham.

Despite the efforts of such men, and despite the labors of such Jesuits as Father Jean Baptiste Menet, the settlements near the mouth of the Tahquamenon were short-lived. The reasons are not obscure. For one thing, the restlessness which prompted natives to find better hunting or fishing was coupled with an inclination to band together with a chief or someone high in their esteem. If a whim prompted him to move, they followed. When he died, they often scattered. With Shegud's death in 1851, Bingham's hopes for a new mission were doomed. Cameron, whose perception of native temperament was perhaps keener than that of his associates, foresaw this; and he also drew attention to the confusion - which often turned into apathy - resulting from the "counteracting exertions" of five religious denominations. The zealous urge to soften the "supreme selfishness of the heathen Indian" (Pitezel's words), or to brighten what Bingham termed "their dark, backslidden state," could make for conflict. Justifiably, the Office of Indian Affairs finally put out a directive admonishing missionaries, here and elsewhere, to stay out of each other's hair.

It was inevitable, also, that relations between native and missionary would not be uniformly cordial. Kaybaynodin plainly tired of a scolding preacher, and when Bingham, who considered strong drink his arch-foe, lectured the chief on its evils, the chief's reply - as the minister quoted it - was dryly pointed:

" 'If my mouth was sewed up, I might possibly keep from it.' "

Bingham then advised him to stay away from its sellers.

" 'Hoh,' said the chief, 'if anybody would cut my legs off, possibly I might.' "

Not without cause was Bingham to decry the "evils of the destructive beverage," or to promote the signing of his temperance pledges. In this, at least, he had the support of Schoolcraft, who complained: "Little does the spirit of commerce care how many Indians die inebriated, if it can be assured of beaver skins." More than a century before, at distant Niagara, local Chippewa had professed their fondness for what, in translation, became "the darling water made by men." Before they had met the European adventurer-trader, their strongest drinks were probably decoctions of gold thread, wild cherry, speckled alder, lady slipper or other plant materials useful for medicine and food. Their introduction to intoxicants - cheap brandy, wine or watered rum - affected them gravely. The improvidence and dependence thus abetted by the persistence of some traders in furnishing it (in spite of their pious denunciations of each other for doing so) will be judged by some to form a squalid chapter in the epoch of discovery and early trade on Lake Superior.

Other reasons for the breakdown of church-supported communities were economic in origin. With the quickening of commerce in the 1850's, especially after the completion of the Sault Canal in 1855, short, seasonal snatches of work became available. Descendants of Shingabawossin and his followers preferred that work cycle rather than depending on their depleted trapping grounds, or to adoption of the agrarian culture urged upon them by the missionaries. Federal financial support of their schools was shortly to be withdrawn. Commercial fishing had been given its impetus by the American Fur Company, and some were catching whitefish and trout for market. Others were attracted to the mill location of James Pendill at Carp River, now known as Pendill's Creek.

Olive Pendill

Olive Pendill

Peter B. Barbeau c. 1855   James P. Pendill c. 1840's

In addition to operating the first sawmill on Whitefish Bay, Pendill employed a cooper to make fish barrels, kept a well-stocked store, and put up wood for the steam vessels then making their appearance on the lake. A gauge of his enterprise is a long inventory of May 1854, showing 250,000 feet of lumber, 2,000 bundles of hay, 280 cords of hardwood, miscellaneous shops and dwellings, store items ranging from dried apples to maple sugar, and from blue muslin to bullet moulds, plus a dock valued at $1,500. To this mill, seeking to arrange for the sawing of dimension timbers, came Charles T. Harvey, the young engineer who superintended the building of the first canal and lock at Sault Ste. Marie.

Late in the 1800's remnants of the Tahquamenon band were to be found in Canada at Batchewana, Goulais Bay and Garden River; and in Michigan chiefly at Iroquois Point or at a location that was to become known as Bay Mills, halfway between Naomikong and the Sault. Well into the present century they gathered from these points to make summer migrations along the shore of the bay or up the river as far as "Squaw Landing" just below the Lower Falls, picking blueberries and cranberries, fishing, and holding camp meetings. Mackinaw sailboats replaced bark canoes, but old ways persisted: the forces of storm were still to be placated by tossing a pinch of tobacco to the waves. Tribal traditions faded; Longfellow's "Hiawatha" took ascendancy over their own fabled heroes.

When Shegud's son Norman died in 1873, the list of his possessions spoke of his generation of natives, its economic lot, its links to the past, with a graphic bleakness: "Deed of Land Containing 88 50/100 acres, One Stove and 4 length of pipe, 3 Elbos, one Tin Kettle, One Boat, one Sail, one Small Canoe, 4 Large Traps and 18 Small Traps, 1 Shotgun. . .9 Nets, 130 Cedar Barks, 200 Sap Dishes, 2 Brass kettles. . .1 New ax, 2 Old Axes. . . ."

Although changed, the role of the church did not end. Father William Gagnieur, a Jesuit known affectionately by Catholics and Protestants alike as the "last of the Black Robes," was one of the best remembered of the missionaries who were to be found at settlements after 1900. By train now, as well as by horse stage or afoot, he visited natives at Salt Point, Shelldrake, Emerson, Eckerman and Trout Lake. Conversant with Chippewa history, he carried on his long labors of devotion and service, with settlers as well, until his death in 1937.

In summary, events between 1830 and 1860 will be seen to have occurred during a period of transition. At its beginning, the Chippewa still lived largely by the hunt, still had technical ownership of most of the land. Before its close they turned grindstones and guided plows. Soon they would face the disturbing mysteries of land patents and deeds. Fully a quarter century before any major attack on the Tahquamenon forest, a saw at Pendill's Creek was ripping boards from the tree that a thinning people called "shingwauk," the pine.

Once you left the shore and went inland, you entered a solitary wilderness. But even here there was a subtle difference. By the fall of 1854, long lines of blazes marched north and south, east and west, across the entire Tahquamenon valley. At intervals there were posts at the bisections of the lines. And nearby there were strange figures carved on the axe-smoothed trunks of trees. Little could the native hunter know, as he peered at those queer markings, that as signs of changing times they were of greater portent than all the omens his ancestors had seen written in the skies.

By Chain and Compass

After one of his axemen had notched the tree properly on both sides coinciding with the line, William Austin Burt opened his rude field book and noted carefully in pencil: "73.12 Cedar 10." The rain persisted; he hunched over to keep it from spotting a page that was slowly filling up with similar cryptic entries. That night, the night of June 18, 1840, he would dry the day's notations in the shelter of his tent. Then he would take pen and ink out of a small box and retrace them for permanence.

Next day he and his assistants would resume the march through the great swamp of the Tahquamenon, toiling with axe and measuring chain and compass to give the surveyor's precise identity to the unknown.

Four years had passed since the people of Michigan, preparing for the statehood that came in 1837, finally agreed to relinquish claim to a narrow strip of land in Ohio for possession of the

William Austin Burt

western Upper Peninsula, an agreement that officially created the state's two-peninsula configuration. For many it was a bitter compromise. Ice-locked in winter, the U.P.'s population scarcely more than a thousand (and these chiefly at the Sault or the Straits of Mackinac), this was soil that held no easy promise. Even when the young state awakened to the riches in ore, timber and fish rimming her northern border, and petitioned Washington for help in building a ship canal at the Sault, the story went around that Henry Clay rose in opposition to speak scornfully of a "place beyond the remotest settlement of the United States, if not in the moon." Native titles to the land were still being extinguished. Except for delineations of the shoreline, the peninsula was unmapped. Such was the country that William Burt entered in the summer of 1840.

A powerfully built man with piercing eyes and shaggy black hair, he brought to his work the practicality of a mill-builder, the ingenuity of an inventor (his solar compass was to prove its worth on countless land surveys), and the unlettered, backwoods wisdom of a circuit-riding judge. His formal schooling in Massachusetts had lasted only six weeks or so, but after turning his hand to varied pursuits near Detroit, he grappled with the principles of surveying and mastered them. In 1833, appointed United States deputy surveyor at forty-one, he began the work that occupied him most of the remainder of his life.

By June 4, 1840, he had crossed the Straits of Mackinac and was in camp about twenty miles northwest of St. Ignace. His prospects for the summer were bleak. Several of his crew, unaccustomed to such forbidding terrain, had left him. Pack horses were next to useless in the "bad and thickety swamps." Mosquitoes swarmed about in clouds. "We now pulverise charcole," he wrote, "and mix a little grees with it and black ourselves.... This is the best remedy that I can find against the Flies."

After picking up crew replacements in the vicinity, Burt turned resolutely northward. In a little more than two weeks he was writing, "Intersect West branch of the Tah-qua-me-naw River," and just below, "as the Indians call it." One phase of the opening up process had begun.

Soon the departure of a sick assistant permitted the sending of a note to his wife, the "Dear Companion" of his infrequent letters. Chiefly he wanted her to know that he and their sons were well, but he also had a request of homely urgency:

> ... I am now more than halfway to Lake Superior from Mackinaw and about 40 or 50 miles from any settlement in the midst of a swamp about twelve miles in diameter but expect to get out tomorrow as I can see high Beech and Maple land to the North & a river between it.... I have just made & launched a Canoe.... My coat & pantiloons are most gone. If you could make me a pair of Pantiloons of the Strongest Kind of Bedticking they would I think stand the Brush....

Reduced to essential terms, his instructions from the surveyor general were simple: Establish a system of township boundaries six miles square according to principles set down in a Continental Congress ordinance of 1785. Here were to be none of the haphazard boundaries of the metes-and-bounds method of surveying common to Colonial America in the eighteenth century. At that time the later retracing of lines was made difficult by descriptions of such parcels of land as the one "called and known by the name of Palm Copplebush, Green Swamp, beginning at the south corner of the patent land formerly belonging to Hendrick Krum, on the edge of said swamp, at a ditch; from thence running south as the compass pointed in the year 1772...." Instead, here was to be a checkerboard pattern of lines laid down at regular intervals, regardless of natural obstacles.

And so the squares took form on Burt's rough maps. Each township lay in relation to another by a series of numbers. The Upper Falls, for example, are located in "town forty-eight north, range eight west," meaning the forty-eighth township north of a base line in Lower Michigan, and the eighth west of a north and south line called the Michigan Meridian, which has its northern terminus at the Sault. In Burt's abbreviated language it became

T48N R8W, and to timber cruisers of a later day, simply "forty-eight, eight." Thus the mouth of the Tahquamenon lies in "forty-eight, six"; the headwaters in "forty-seven, twelve," one tier of townships south and six ranges west. Strictly speaking, north and south lines are range lines; those running east and west at the same six-mile intervals are township, or town, lines. Together, they describe township boundaries.

For parts of two summers William Burt tramped the river country, accompanied by a crew that included three of his sons, Austin, John and Wells. At least ten times they crossed the river itself, setting "meander" posts on each bank to mark the points of intersection. Altogether they measured and marked some 550 miles of lines between the southern reaches of Tahquamenon tributaries and Lake Superior.

Since they were compelled to travel light, their provisions consisted chiefly of a few staples: flour, salt pork, beans, dried apples, rice, tea and coffee, a small amount of "saleratus" (baking soda), sugar and salt. A tent or two, mackinaw blankets, a few tin utensils, and the surveying equipment were their other major necessities. Before lake navigation ended in the fall they returned to the Lower Peninsula, Burt to make clean copies of his maps and those indispensable records, the field notes. By the end of November he fulfilled his contract by reporting to the surveyor general at Cincinnati. He received $4.25 per mile of line. It was meager enough payment, even then, for he had to pay his assistants - two chainmen, two axemen, a packer and a cook - out of his own pocket.

On August 28, 1841, he completed the township enclosing the headwaters of the Tahquamenon. Succeeding summers took him out of the watercourse and westward to his discovery of iron ore near Marquette in 1844, and later, to the establishment of the Michigan-Wisconsin boundary. One of America's abler pioneers, William Austin Burt had been eminently worthy of his hire. Across the entire valley of the Tahquamenon, as they had where Milwaukee now stands, and as they had across prairie land in Iowa, his lines ran well-marked and true.

To break this land up into smaller parcels or "descriptions" was the task that remained. A few surveyors, among them Wells Burt, accomplished much of this by subdividing each township into mile-square, numbered sections during the summers of 1849-1854. The numbering began with 1 in the northeast corner of the township, thence west to section 6. Section 7 joined it on the south; section 12 joined section 1 on the south, and so on back and forth, ending with section 36 in the southeast (on a map, the lower righthand) corner.

For the uninitiated, the field notes of these surveys are apt to be nothing more than a mass of weird figures and symbols. Their very brevity is puzzling. Once deciphered, however, they reveal in concise fashion both the methods used and the appearance of the country at the time.

The standard basis of measurement in all instances was a 66-foot chain of 100 links, each 7.92 inches in length. All distances were expressed in terms of chains and links. An even eighty chains made a mile.

By the time Wells Burt was subdividing in 1850, it was customary to run each interior line of a township twice. Under this plan of ensuring accuracy, the first line was called a "random." Only on the corrected line were the corners fixed. Like his father, ten years before, he was required to establish corners for each section and for each quarter section. Theoretically, his section corners would be nearly eighty chains apart, with the "quarter posts" halfway between; but in practice, the length of each line was inclined to vary a little. There were several reasons for this, including slight differences in measurement and the necessity of "closing" at the corners already set in the 1840 and 1841 surveys.

Here now is Wells Burt in action. He is working on the north and south section line that crosses the Tahquamenon just above the Upper Falls. The random line, run north, has been finished. His field book entries for it, with distances in the left-hand column in chains and links, are complete.

North Random between Secs. 11 & 12. Var. 2 40' E
4.00   Enter Swamp Course S.W.
17.00   Leave Swamp S.W.
40.00   Set temporary post
49.75   Portage trail Course E & W
54.00   Descend hill 40 feet to river
55.43   Intersect right bank of Tah-qua-me-naw river
*   and set temporary post*
57.62   Over river to left bank and set temporary post
61.50   Top of hill 40 feet high

80.00 Set temporary post cor. to Secs. 1, 2, 11 & 12
Land level - soil sandy. Timber: Sugar, Hemlock, Fir, etc.
Line run by the needle. Var. 2 40' E

The last line tells us that the sky is so overcast that his solar compass, requiring an observation of the sun, has been put aside. He is using instead the common surveyor's compass fitted with open sights.

Now he is ready to project a corrected line south. Let us go with him to observe his procedure on the latter half of this distance. Having determined that the finished line will be seventy-nine chains and seventy-eight links in length, Burt stops at the halfway mark. A hard (sugar) maple post is squared and set in the ground. Next he selects what is to become a "witness tree," or, more properly a bearing tree. A yellow birch stands just southwest of the post. On the side facing the corner, one of the axemen makes a large blaze. Using a timber scribe, an ingeniously contrived little cutting tool, he cuts across the face of the blaze the legend "1/4S" to indicate that this is a quarter-section corner. Then he makes a short, lengthwise blaze just above the ground, and inscribes the letters "BT" for "bearing tree." A horizontal notch is cut below the letters, the distance from it to the corner post is measured, and its compass bearing from the post is determined. After another bearing tree on the opposite side of the line has been marked, Burt makes this entry:

39.89 Set Sugar qr. Sec. post from which A Y. Birch
11 in. dia. bears S48W 11 lks dist. & A Sugar
11 in. dia. bears N40E 2 lks dist.

Long after the post at the actual corner has rotted away at the ground and toppled, these two trees, one standing 48 degrees west of south, the other 40 degrees east of north, will bear the true point silent witness.

Burt goes south again, guiding his axemen through the compass sights. Carefully now, for an error might mean starting over, the chainmen follow with their measurement, the lead man setting tally pins a chain apart, his partner picking them up. Soon a tree looms up fairly in the line of sight. Directed by Burt, an axeman pauses to cut two notches on each side. Its distance from the preceding section corner, its species and diameter are noted.

(Such "line" or "sight" trees still perform the service of revealing the location of a line. They are useful aids, also, when it becomes necessary to locate a corner at which the bearing trees have disappeared.)

Another line tree is recorded before Burt reaches the end:

67.40   a Sugar 13 in. dia.

His last entry gives the bearing trees at the section corner:

79.78   Set Hemlock post cor. to Secs. 11, 12, 13, & 14
From which A W. Pine 8 in. dia. bears N35E 21 lks dist &
A Hemlock 14 in. dia. bears South 2 lks. dist.

The bearing tree marks here are made in much the same fashion as at the quarter corner, except that each tree receives the township number, range number, and the number of the section on which it stands. Thus the first tree is inscribed "T48N R8W S12."

So the men of William Burt's calling ran their lines - clambering up the sides of gullies, hacking through windfalls, floundering with their measuring chains across sloughs; and always they left behind those unique signboards engraved in solid wood. Into the notes went references to timber and soil types, streams and trails, traces of settlement. Cranberry marshes were considered worthy of comment, and wherever there was much hard maple, there was often mention of native sugar-making. Subdividing the township that includes Naomikong Point, Harvey Mellen drew attention to the natives living on the lakeshore. Of the township in general he wrote, "I think that it offers many inducements to the actual settler." Wells Burt, on the other hand, after struggling through alder thickets about

H.C. Lawrence

Harold C. Lawrence, veteran surveyor.

C.G. Taylor

Original bearing tree for Sec. 7, T50N R7W, set Sept. 18, 1849, by Wells Burt. New corner set July, 1966.

ten miles east of the site of Newberry, closed his notes with an acid reflection that the whole township was worthless.

Reports of bog iron ore not far from Newberry gave rise to rumors of rich deposits that were to furnish dreams for visionaries until the turn of the century. "Enter burnt land" was a fairly common entry, especially for lines crossing pine stands north of the river. One surveyor reported a good mill site about six miles below the headwaters. Another, working in the falls area, noted that the river was capable of furnishing "a vast amount of water power."

Hundreds of miles of Tahquamenon lines have been retraced and their corners re-established in the present century. Surveyors Harold Lawrence and Jim Cook, working from Newberry in the 1920's and 1930's, spent years at this valuable restoration, fixing lost corners with a skill that would have been admired by the pioneer men whose steps they followed.

Although doomed to eventual disappearance, many trees in the Tahquamenon country still bear the old telltale scribe marks, all or partially hidden now beneath their annual rings of growth. One of these is a favorite of mine.

When the right-of-way for state highway M-28 was cleared across the boundary between Luce and Chippewa Counties, a section corner dating from William Burt's survey lay in its path. The bearing trees were destroyed. But not far away is a gnarled cedar line tree. Now and then as I pass by I throw a salute its way. Small homage, indeed, to pay the memory of the purposeful man who paused beside it to open his field book on that distant day in 1840, when the rain slanted across the swamp, as if to erase his spare record - "73.12 Cedar 10."

Five-Log Pine

For more than forty years the thudding of axes resounded through Tahquamenon pine.

The river lay in a swath of the great Michigan harvest that remained confined to the middle of the Lower Peninsula until shortly after the Civil War. Then men swung it north and west, irresistibly, in a long arc. Sooner than was thought possible, it merged with similar onslaughts on the northern Wisconsin and Minnesota pineries.

There was as yet no railroad, no permanent settlement in the valley when the first big sticks floated against booms near the mouth of the river. Surveyor William Burt's bearing tree marks were still plain to the eye; bark canoes had not yet completely disappeared from the portages. After its start in the early 1870's, the principal cut gained momentum speedily a decade later, and was declining by 1900. If one takes into account the logs produced on the smaller, neighboring river systems - Shelldrake (or Betsy), Two Hearted, and Sucker - the yield will be found to have exceeded a billion feet of white pine alone. In addition, millions of feet of Norway, or red, pine, the smaller and less valuable species, were sent to market from stands on the nearby Lake Superior shore.

It appears to be true that the first major cut of the valley's pine was made by George Dawson of Sault Ste. Marie, who had a partnership arrangement with Calvin & Breck, a Canadian firm located at Kingston, Ontario, near the entrance to the turbulent St. Lawrence River. Down the St. Lawrence these square-hewn logs, called waney board timber, were eventually rafted to the port of Quebec for shipment by schooner to Great Britain. Of all the products of the Tahquamenon woods, none reached its final destination against hazards of such degree.

George Dawson started in the Upper Peninsula in 1871, after getting into the squared-timber business in Canada. According to a biographical sketch published in 1911, he was " ... among the first to institute lumbering operations at Two Hearted River, Grand Marais and Tahquamenon River, and later on Drummond Island in 1880." He also bought waterfront property at the village of De Tour where the Dawson Subdivision takes up the central area. In 1877 he built an imposing residence in Sault Ste. Marie, where streets have been named for him and his wife Carrie.

George Dawson.

Dawson Creek carries his name in northern Luce County in a vicinity where he took out timber.

Dawson brought on the scene the board timber men, to introduce a phase of Tahquamenon lumbering that owed its origins more to Canada than to Lower Michigan. If the era knew hardy, self-reliant men, there were those who said that one of the best of them was a Dawson foreman, David (Big Dave) Ranson, who had moved north from Canada's Ottawa

River in 1868. He worked with a crew made up largely of French Canadians, quick on their feet, quick with song or jest, adept with axes. Around their waists they wore scarlet sashes, more decorative than useful, marking the red sash brigade. As they moved eastward along the shore of Lake Superior from the dunes of Grand Marais to Waiska Bay, they fashioned long hewn timbers for shipment abroad.

Will Ranson

David ("Big Dave") Ranson.

See David Ranson now as he selects new timber in the Tahquamenon hinterland. Here is no massive pine forest, unbroken for mile after mile, as in some Michigan stands; but where it grows, benefiting often from the protection of interspersed hardwoods, it is of prime quality. And only the choicest trees, of course, are to fall in the beginning. As yet there are no local mills - this product is destined for remanufacture in England.

So he hunts it, his burly shoulders carrying the strain of his pack, his eyes busy with the "lay" of the ridges, the types and amounts of timber. Sometimes when the pine thins, he fastens on a pair of tree climbers, spots the next dark maze of tops, and takes a course for it. After a month or more of this searching, alone or with a single helper "running compass," he has the location of another year's operation fixed in his mind: the sites for camps, the landing for supplies, the best locations for sleigh and tote roads. In the waning summer and through crisp days when beechnuts are dropping and tamaracks are shedding their needles, noises of preparation will echo through the woods. Then after the long winter work is over, after the river ice rots in the spring, herded timbers will go down to Lake Superior to be loaded into ports in the sterns of vessels bound for Lower Canada.

"It was considerable of an undertaking," wrote an early operator, "to load that timber in ships, carry it to Kingston,

Ontario, discharge it and make it up into big rafts, run them through the St. Lawrence rapids past Montreal, then tow the rafts to Quebec, break them up, load them into sailing ships for Liverpool, England, put them up in small rafts to go through the small canal to Manchester as that was before the ship canal was built." Few are the Tahquamenon lumbermen of today, concerned as they may be with the sale of lesser products, or bedeviled by mechanical failures, or snagged on the newfangledness of strict record-keeping, who would deny that this amounted, at the least, to "considerable of an undertaking."

Judged by present-day concepts of utilization, the board timber operators of that period were prodigals in an already wasteful industry. After a single length had been hewn, half the volume of a tree might be left behind. "It was a massacring of the forests," said the renowned Robert Dollar, another local producer, as he looked back across five decades from the vantage point of a West Coast shipping magnate in 1929. "They all did it in those days, and so did I, but it never was right." But like the harried lumberman of a more recent day who complained, "If my foresight was only as good as my hindsight," we may find it too easy now to peer down the trusty barrels of second-guess and to take potshots at the "timber barons" or the "despoilers of the forest." Possibly, in the 1875-1905 economy in which "laissez-faire" was the rule, and conservation still only a vague word, squandering was inevitable. The mood of a lumber-hungry nation fostered a quick gleaning. "Let's give 'er tarpaper, boys!" was the call to harvest. Far into the green distance loomed the challenge of "five-log pine," a run averaging five logs to a thousand board feet. That it ever should be gone was once beyond envisaging.

At the tree itself a board timber crew most often consisted of four: two "fallers," or timber fitters, a scorer and a hewer. Some gangs worked together for many seasons, and although practices varied, the hewer often was boss of it, taking pay on a piecework basis.

After the fallers had cut down a selected tree and sawed the trunk into proper length - butting off any signs of rot and often stopping short of the first limb - they marked it where it would "make" with a chalked line. Thus guided, the third man stood on it, notched into its sides ("score-hackin' ") at short intervals and split out the chunks with his axe, being careful not to chop inside the line. Equipped with his heavy broadaxe, which he wielded as deftly as a champion fly caster whips his rod, the hewer now took his turn, moving alongside the timber from either end, and keeping the heel of the axe down as he hewed squarely on the line. His offset handle enabled him to work from the ground, rather than on the stick, as was the later custom in hewing cedar and tamarack ties. As he went forward into the cut, "scissoring off" rough edges left by the scorer, he left a surface almost as smooth as a planed board. If he happened to be on a slope, this feat could be a tricky one indeed, for he had to prevent a natural tendency to "wedge" in or out with his strokes. Two sides finished, they turned the timber over and the process was repeated.

Formerly pine had been hewn perfectly square (crews boasted of "the four proud edges"), but some loss was prevented in Tahquamenon trees by making what was called waney pine. It was only partly squared - broad, slightly rounded corners called "wanes" were left, from which the bark was removed. These edges usually varied because of the taper of the tree or a bend in it. An allowance of a taper of about two inches for each twenty feet of finished timber also reduced wastage to some extent.

Payment for board timber was based on cubic measure. In a transaction of 1888, David Ranson contracted to produce it near the present community at Strongs Corners. The pieces were to average not less than twenty-one inches square, "string or over," and not less than twenty-five feet in length. He agreed to accept a total of twenty-two and a half cents per cubic foot for 20,000 feet delivered to the stern of a vessel in the Straits of Mackinac. Interim payments were to be typically scattered: five cents per cubic foot when the timbers were on skids, five cents when on cars of the newly built railroad, five cents when unloaded at St. Ignace, and the remainder when shipped.

Like many who followed his calling with the same initiative, Ranson was first a camp foreman, with the duties of timber cruiser thrown in. While he was bossing crews for George Dawson, pioneer Sault lumberman, he entered Tahquamenon Bay and built a crib dock near Kaybaynodin's deserted village. There he cut a tote trail, to be known as the East and West Road, from the shore to a point on the river about ten miles above the Upper Falls. Later, he had a contract with shrewd John Spry, Chicago lumber and land dealer, for furnishing 18 million feet of logs each year to the Spry mill in the Sault. During the 1890's the two collaborated on land deals. Ranson knew the Tahquamenon country; Spry knew men who wanted its pine. It was an ideal combination of talents.

In *A Saga of the St. Lawrence*, his 1945 history of the family business, D.D. Calvin says that the chief reason for the purchase of pine by Calvin & Breck was that pine was necessary to float rafts of the heavy oak which the Canadian firm brought to its Kingston center at Garden Island from the oak forests of Ontario, Ohio and southern Michigan. However, a company letter of July 11, 1879, instructs: " ... suggest your not using any at all of either Dawson's or Carrier's pine for floating oak - using such good timber to float oak is a losing game."

The correspondence between George Dawson, Calvin & Breck, and the D.D. Calvin Company (the Quebec office) indicates their concern about a multiplicity of problems in the securing of cutters and supplies, clearing of snow-roads, river-driving of logs, and "making" of timber to the desired specifications. In October of 1876, Dawson wrote the firm from "Camp":

> I am getting along very well, have about 50,000 feet made of good timber and well mfgd. I am not leaving as much wane as I have been in the habit of doing. The water is too low this fall to run any timber over them but I am confident that I will have no trouble. We are now blasting the rock on the falls and am making a good job of it. I think and am in hopes the timber will suit next season. I am now working four gangs til Jan. 1....

On November 11, 1876, Hiram Calvin replied: "I ... hope you are right in your belief that you will have no trouble running the Tahquamenon." His letter goes on in regard to payment of some of the workmen, who lived in crude shanties and were furnished a spare diet: "Of those who were to receive a round amount for the winter, I have given Charles LeCroix $10 the whole amount which he is entitled to get - I have given Frank Couriveau $4, to receive next $4 on 1st Jan'y...."

Dawson's association with the Calvin interests ended in 1879, after a disastrous incident that winter involving his French Canadian crew. Before the end of the cutting season several of the men returned home to Quebec suffering from frostbite. They had been frostbitten as they crossed the ice of Tahquamenon Bay on foot headed for Sault Ste. Marie, Michigan. One had died. They alleged that Dawson had turned them out of his camp. Some of them brought suit for damages against the D.D. Calvin Company, and, though the suit failed, the widely publicized affair was distressing for all the participants.

Timbers were shipped out as usual that spring. Calvin & Breck notified Dawson by letter on June 10, 1879:

> The Schooners *Norway* and *Siberia* left here this afternoon to load for you. The *Norway* will go to the Taquamenon direct. Please give Capt. Dix instructions at the Sault exactly where to go to load and give him as good dispatch as you can. The *Siberia* will go to Grand Marais and load what you have there then return to Taquamenon to finish. Please put on an extra heavy crew and rush her along in order that she may not lose her place. ... If any instructions for *Siberia* address Capt. J. O'Brien, Sault Ste. Marie.

The dangerous technique of "lake shore loading" had to be used for that part of the timber not near enough to a stream to float it out to deep and sheltered water - timber brought over snow-roads and left on the beach. D.D. Calvin described the operation:

> Sounding as they went, the vessels would feel their way in, anchoring as close to shore as was prudent. Boats were lowered, and long "lake shore lines" run from vessel to beach. The timber-men would set the timber afloat, the vessel-men then "dogged" it together, a few pieces at a time. To reach their vessels, they stood or sat on each little lot of timber and hauled it out by means of the "lake shore line." ... Loading and stowing several hundred heavy, slippery pieces of timber was a unique form of hard work, bearing no resemblance whatever to the mechanical loading of the usual bulk cargo of the Great Lakes - wheat, coal, iron ore.... Timber went first through ports into the hold, then over-side to be piled on deck. "All and sundry the dangers of navigation," as they were summed up in Bills of Lading, constantly intrude upon the story of Lake navigation.

Queen's University Archives, Kingston, Ontario

Lake barge "Ceylon" and square-hewn timbers at Garden Island, Ontario.

Although their lumbering operations in northern Michigan ended in 1879, and they disposed of their extensive land holdings in 1882, the schooners, tugs and barges of Calvin & Breck continued to carry Tahquamenon pine through the Great Lakes. In 1885 Robert Dollar wrote to engage ships: "We have enough timber made now so I am sure of 3 trips for 5 vessels of 117 M per trip." On July 12, 1896, J. & W. Flatt wrote: " ... to advise you as to quantity of Pine to be removed from Michigan, which is as follows: 45,000 at Emerson, Lake Superior... ."

The Flatt brothers, based in Hamilton, Ontario, spread their large camps from Newberry to Shingleton, to Sidnaw, and as far west as Ashland, Wisconsin. In his memoirs, *The Trail of Love*, William D. Flatt said of his site near Newberry:

> Our camps were started here with 300 men and 75 teams. The cutting was easy but the skidding difficult... . We had about 45 miles of road, and it was here that we proved the value of ice roads. We ran both day and night crews, the snowplows and sprinklers being operated by one lot of men at night and the hauling being done by day ... over the snow roads we would have averaged about 1,500 feet to the

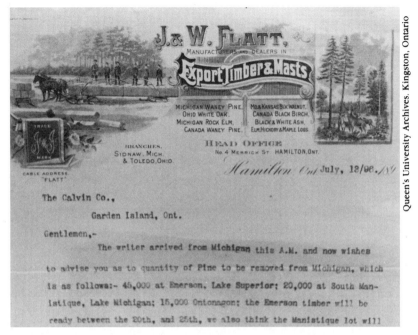

The vessels of the Calvin Company carried the timber of the Flatts from Michigan sites, including Emerson at the mouth of the Tahquamenon.

load ... as it was we carried an average of over 6,000 feet per load. At this camp and over these roads we hauled the largest load of waney board timber ever carried in Northern Michigan....

This may have been the one described in *The Newberry News* of March 2, 1894, under the heading "A Big Load." It was made up of ten pieces of waney board timber hauled by one team for one and one-half miles, and scaled 31,304 feet board measure.

On March 16 of that same year the *News* reported that J. & W. Flatt had rented "Mr. Louck's large scow which he recently fitted up as a floating camp, for the purpose of accommodating the men looking after the drive." W.D. Flatt, who declared the Tahquamenon "probably the most difficult stream to drive in Northern Michigan," accompanied the drive that year and highlighted the experience in his book. In only one long day, all the banked timbers were rolled into the river, creating "a solid jam of over five miles in length." The drive to Lake Superior took

Mrs. D.N. McLeod

Board timber produced by D.N. McLeod (hand on flatcar).

twenty-six days. Of the scene at the Upper Falls, Flatt said: "to me the Whirlpool Rapids at Niagara seem tame compared with this. While watching our timber shoot through the rapids we would see timber two feet square broken up like matches. I remember remarking to the men that we must be losing $2,500 a minute in broken timber at this spot."

D.N. (Dan) McLeod, who came to Newberry in 1885 as a hotel proprietor, took one of his first local woods jobs for the Flatts. There was an early thaw and W.D. Flatt promised him the best coat in Canada if he got the timber out. Cold weather returned; McLeod hauled at night, and later sported a magnificent Persian lamb.

After big sawmills appeared in the 1880's, shipments of "squared stuff" declined, but did not end until about 1913. The weathered residues of long butts and chips, while they lasted, marked the presence of some of the most dexterous of America's outdoor workmen.

Meanwhile the tide of private ownership rose. In the big record books of the Chippewa County Register of Deeds at the Sault (and in Newberry, after Luce County was formed in 1887), hand-filled pages testified to the variety of purchasers. Speculators, tax title buyers, land jugglers intent on one trade or another, colonizers, applicants for title under the "Timber and Stone" Act of 1878, lumbermen by the score - all appeared on the new buying frontier. And with them came a sprinkling of homesteaders and settlers, whose modest entries speak still of hard-won little clearings, most of which, north of the river at least, have only an apple tree or faint trace of foundation remaining to remind one of man's dogged trysting with the land.

The buyers of most of it were dealers in land or timber. One of these was Francis Palms, the Belgian who managed an empire of land single-handed from his modest home in Detroit. "All the old-time lumbermen of Michigan," says a biographer, "helped wear down the paving stones that led from the street to Francis Palms' office." Others of prominence were Franklin Moore, another Detroiter, and Russell A. Alger, Abijah Weston, David Whitney and William B. Mershon. The Civil War was not long past; there were also Bay City's Henry W. Sage, who had sold timbers for the Union pontoon crossing of the Rappahannock; and Alonzo Chesbrough, a onetime producer of oak shipknees in Ohio, who was credited with furnishing timbers to back up the steel plates of that historic gunboat, the *Monitor.*

Fortunes of an even earlier war, the War of 1812, added illuminating postscripts to some of the first conveyances. At the beginning, almost all of the land in the valley was open for entry at the U.S. Land Office in Marquette for $1.25 an acre. Yet another method of gaining possession, that of using bounty land warrants, was also in favor. This scrip, as the warrants were loosely called, had been issued by a government poor in money but rich in land as a bonus for its veterans of the War of 1812. Readily negotiable after 1852, the bounty land warrants - usually good for 160 acres each - might be bought up from the veteran or his heirs, or from dealers in eastern states. Hence wads of "BLWs," as well as cash, found their way to the land agent at Marquette. Thus men such as William Elliott, "Private, Captain Rodney's Company, Delaware Militia, War 1812," had their names remotely attached to land they never saw. His was a quarter section known by sight to thousands who have traveled the river, for it enclosed - after the primary lumbering was over - the familiar landmark of McNearney Farm.

In the pine woods fraternity the man who answered to the synonymous names of timber cruiser or landlooker was in a skillful, if inconspicuous, class by himself. He was, they said, "a bush hound two jumps ahead of a lumberjack."

He belonged by right to the trail blazers of a continent. To appraise stands of timber - for speculation or logging - was his basic job. More than most woodsmen, he worked in a position of trust. The fate of a small fortune often depended upon the accuracy of his estimates, the soundness of his judgment. His qualifications set him at the forefront of the heyday that was to come. He knew how to judge quality in trees, and how to estimate accurately their content in board measure; how to keep track of distance on uneven land by pacing; how to read survey notes so as to know his location on any "description"; how to adjust for the ever-changing magnetic variation of the pull at his compass needle; and with a logger's practicality, how to assess the costs and risks of production.

Of the many men who "looked" Tahquamenon pine - such as Charles Metcalf, John Gleason, Frank Weston, David Ranson and his son Will, Francis Hulbert and his sons Richard and John, Ambro Bettes, John and Robert Hunter - some were in the employ of others at a monthly wage. A few free-lanced, selling the notes they made; others, having enough capital or backing, went on their own, trading in timber or engaging in lumbering. If a large tract were involved, a party of cruisers and compass men, as many as seven or eight, might take to the woods. In 1897, when nearly all the pine was in private ownership, Will Ranson spent five months with such a crew in the eastern part of the waterway, exploring some 30,000 acres.

Timber cruising party, c. 1904, on Wire Road north of Eckerman.

As a rule, it was work that lacked the excitement of the

W.D. Hulbert

river drive, the color of logging camp life. Once the corners had been located, and a starting point established, the daily ritual of pacing through each forty and filling in the estimate blanks at night became tinged with monotony. Yet it was a monotony mixed with newness, too, for the woods were full of strange quirks of happenstance, like meeting a lynx crouched over his kill, or watching the placid movements of a porcupine feeding in the top of a hemlock. Signs in the snow were commonplace to the cruiser; reading the story of the tracks was as easy for him as reading a map. And all day his keen eye took in the timber, the lay of the land. Crossing streams as yet unnamed, the Murphy, Gimlet, Teaspoon, Riley, Linton or Cheney, he would pause for a drink, often scooping it up in the curled brim of a battered hat that bore a distinct resemblance to weathered tarpaper. Then a smoke, perhaps, and a glance at his compass, and he resumed his pacing.

So it was largely solitary work, and often highly competitive: first come, first served at the land office. Finding the snowshoe tracks of another cruiser near Salt Point in the 1870's, Francis Hulbert raced south to the shore of Lake Michigan, west to a railroad, and beat his rival to Marquette. His was the kind of experience that was to be repeated, no less spectacularly, before the pine gave out.

Traveling light could be a paramount necessity. From Hulbert's son Richard, who had worked at the problem of sustaining strength miles from civilization, comes this matter-of-fact description of a typical menu when food for his helpers was carried in packsacks:

> For breakfast, dried fruit stewed with sugar, if you wanted it. Bacon. Eggs the first few days. Toast or hot cakes. Sometimes you would warm up a few navy beans that had been left over from the day before. Coffee. We did not come back to our tent for lunch, but carried it in leather pouches slung over our backs. I would often make sandwiches as follows: bread and butter, and between the slices of bread fried bacon with raspberry jam. These with a few dried figs or raisins would be enough. I had a small oval-shaped pail made that I could put in my lunch bag, and we would often take that along in winter. If the weather was cold at noon, we would build a fire, melt some snow and have a cup of

hot tea. For supper there would be navy beans or perhaps
pea soup or rice, bread and butter or biscuits or corn bread
baked in a reflector, dried fruit and tea or coffee. I could
keep in pretty good condition on that kind of diet.

A truly Spartan fare, in contrast, was that of an old landlooker
who scorned variety, and who boasted that he could prepare his
breakfast in seven minutes after he crawled out of his blankets.
His meal consisted of salt pork, bread and coffee. The pork, it
should be noted, was not always cooked.

"It is in autumn," said William Davenport Hulbert, the writer
son of Francis, "that the landlooker is in clover." Mosquitoes, deer
flies and the obnoxious "no-see-ums" were gone; the absence
of foliage made it easier to follow a blazed line or to fix one's sight
on a distant, looming tree. Early summer cruising was something
else again. Fifty years after Burt led his survey parties of the
1840's, insects remained a plague; but the Tahquamenon
woodsman now substituted for grease and charcoal a pungent
repellent of fat rubbed with oil of tar. You could tell a cruiser
anywhere, by the stain around his hip pocket. It was still handy
to carry a chunk of pork rind there.

In winter the concave trail of his snowshoes traced regular
patterns beneath the soaring branches. Intruding on the stillness
("so quiet sometimes you could hear it"), the blow of an axe, or
the muffled creaking of snowshoes after a pause, turned into
crescendos of sound. But complete solitariness was passing. As
he described a party making camp north of Eckerman in 1905,
William Hulbert was reminded that his father, alone in the
country thirty years before, "had often bivouacked in the snow,
in the coldest weather of a Lake Superior winter, without even
a tent between him and the stars, but with only a little square of
cotton on sticks at the head of his bed to break the wind." Now
toboggans were in use, and tents, and collapsible sheet-iron stoves
equipped with telescoping pipes.

Denied a strenuous life in the woods by a crippling childhood
illness, William Hulbert chronicled episodes of the Tahquamenon
pine era for magazines. From his own family, as from other
landlookers and lumbermen, he drew many details. On canoe
trips and on laborious walks, laden with a heavy camera of the
time, he absorbed others.

Turning now from his naturalist's bent for wildlife stories, he

Forest Neighbors by W.D. Hulbert.

pondered the fate of this remaining overstory of majestic trees. He had traced their growth from cone-covered seed to a maturity "of rugged strength and grandeur"; he knew the crashing sureness of their fall. In words that remain epitaphic, he took leave of the pines, writing that by night:

The moon and the stars kept watch over them, just as they had done for so many, many years, and when the wind blew upon their branches they lifted up their voices in the old, old hymn that their family had sung through all the ages. The world was as beautiful as ever, and there seemed to be no reason why it should not go on so to all eternity. And yet something had happened. Man, the great enemy of all pine trees, had been there, and though he had gone away he would surely come again. Sooner or later the lumberman follows the landlooker, and when the lumberman has finished his work the glory of the woods is gone....

The Newberry News.

Milltowns and the Waterway

It was apparent by the 1870's that development in Michigan's Upper Peninsula warranted the construction of a railroad from St. Ignace to Marquette to connect with the one being pushed northward to the Straits of Mackinac. The syndicate formed to build it included John S. Newberry and four other prominent Detroit men of the period - Francis Palms, George Hendrie, F.E. Driggs and William B. Moran - and three Eastern capitalists, among them a man who gave his name to Seney, a place of lurid reputation in the pine days. Known as the Detroit, Mackinac & Marquette Railroad, it was completed in 1881. After some consolidations with other lines, and after the branch from Soo Junction to the Sault was finished in 1887, it was given the unwieldy name of Duluth, South Shore and Atlantic Railway Company (DSS&A). Smoke had hardly cleared from the muzzles of the guns at the Sault's Fort Brady, welcoming the first train,

Wayne Moulton

DSS&A (South Shore) Locomotive "50" and Billy Kendall, 1912.

when a local wit dubbed it "Damned Slow Service and Abuse." (Its employees said "Darn Small Salary and Abuse"). Commonly known simply as "The South Shore" for more than seventy years, it was merged into the Soo Line Railroad in the early 1960's.

Newberry

Meanwhile, in 1882, some of the Detroit men interested in the railroad established the Vulcan Furnace Company for making charcoal iron, and the village of Newberry sprang up around it. It was platted, streets were laid out, and in 1885 it was incorporated, at that time a part of Chippewa County. Vice-president of the furnace company was John S. Newberry, for whom the village was named, though it was just "Grant's Camp" in 1880, when twenty-year-old pioneer Matt Surrell, Sr., traveled to the railroad construction site by wagon from Naubinway on Lake Michigan. He and his team were soon hauling supplies, and before long his livery provided transportation by stage and cutter. Other businesses usually found in a north-woods place were installed, as well as churches and the beginnings of a school system. The principal street names assigned then were those of various members of the Newberry family, none of whom ever lived here. Newberry and Truman, Helen, John, Harrie, Handy, Parmelee, Phelps and Robinson - so they remain today. An exception was in the naming of McMillan Avenue for James

Charles Beaulieu

Newberry Avenue, c. 1890, looking south from railroad tracks of DSS&A.

McMillan, who, like Truman Newberry afterwards, was shortly to serve the people of Michigan as United States Senator. In 1887, when Luce County - named for Cyrus B. Luce, then governor of Michigan - was organized and set off from its neighbors, Newberry became the seat of county government.

The furnace company put up long rows of company houses and built a company store. For many years it was the economic mainstay of the village, employing - at the plant and in its surrounding woods operations - as many as five or six hundred men. In 1890 its production capacity was reported as 75 gross tons of charcoal pig iron a day. The "pigs" were corded up by grade, ninety pounds each, and stacked by hand. Much of this tonnage went to St. Ignace by rail to be loaded on boats for shipment to manufacturers of railroad car wheels.

Hardwood, cut by the cord into four-foot lengths, was brought from the surrounding forests for the making of charcoal in the kilns which stood like ranks of giant brick beehives. In one week in June 1886, 31,899 bushels of charcoal were required for the production of 329 tons of pig iron. Locally quarried limestone was used to separate the dross in the hearth - 200 pounds of stone to each ton of raw ore - which came by rail from the Marquette range.

The industry did extensive railroad logging in the central part of the Tahquamenon valley, in the 1890's building its first line, a narrow-gauge, southeast to the vicinity of the present county airport. One running northwesterly from Newberry was started

Grant Bros. postcard view of Newberry, c. 1910. The furnace company's charcoal kilns are in foreground.

about 1903, the two running out of McMillan were active about 1915, and the main line going northeasterly from Newberry was pushed in that direction in 1926, to the company's last main camp on the west side of the Tahquamenon, Camp 8.

The furnace knew many shutdowns, changes of name, and reorganizations. An expansion beginning in 1910 added the production of lumber and chemicals, chiefly acetic acid to be used in the manufacture of paint and rayon fabric. A retort plant replaced the old kilns. In the twenty retorts, buggies of wood were subjected to intense heat and the chemical liquor removed, after which the residual charcoal was transferred to coolers. The memorable scene of "pulling retorts" was recorded by Merle Fretz in an editorial in *The Newberry News*:

> In our day pulling time was marked by the appearance of Dick Beach, Sr. and his gang ... mostly huge, powerful Finns ... .
>
> First the keys were knocked out of the heavy iron retort door, and it was a sight to behold those big fellows swinging heavy sledges like tack hammers. As the last key fell, other men swung the door aside. The inrushing air ignited the gases and the charcoal, and the opening door resembled nothing so much as the yawning gates of hell. Gas and unbearable heat enveloped the men ... .

The ripple of smooth muscles on powerful frames of men, who in one flaming moment ceased to be men but became sweating gods of fire, their precision of movement, their sublime disregard of heat, weight and fatigue, their look of victory as the burning buggies moved smoothly out and the cooler doors closed upon their threat, made an unforgettable sight.

Philip S. Hamilton, who started employment there in 1912, became manager of the works in 1929, a position he retained until 1945, when operations came to an end. Known then as the Newberry Lumber and Chemical Company, it was the last plant in the Midwest to make charcoal iron.

Principally a furnace town in its beginning, Newberry was also an outfitting place for scores of lumber companies and their camps in the first thirty years of its existence. It was the gateway north to the Deer Park country, and in the spring when the log drives were in, it both suffered and entertained a concentration of lumberjacks as tough as whang-leather. Saloon license fees for a long while paid most, if not all, of the costs of running the village government.

The columns of *The Newberry News* in those early years reveal

Matt Surrell

Barroom, McLeod House, c. 1890's, with D.N. McLeod behind the counter.

C.G. Taylor

Former home of D.N. McLeod, built in 1898 by John A. Shattuck.

that there were often (as the editor put it) "lively times in the village." But it must not be thought that saloons or rambunctiousness provided the only entertainment in the woodland society. For instance, during the week of April 5, 1888, the *News* noted these activities: a presentation of *Uncle Tom's Cabin*, a "literary and musical," a production of *H.M.S. Pinafore*, and a program by the Hicks-Sawyer minstrels. There were boating excursions, sleigh rides and hay rides, visiting lecturers (like the famed Miss Frances Willard, who spoke on the evils of drink), and an assortment of traveling strong men, balloon ascensionists and horse racers to watch and mingle with.

The first issue of *The Newberry News* greeted the public on June 10, 1886, after a group of local businessmen bought a print shop and named Clyde W. Hecox as editor. It was a five-column four-page paper, two pages made up locally and two of "boiler plate" sent up each week from Detroit. The country was opening up and nobody hesitated to brag about it. The paper was full of such items as how a couple of men felled a tree and cut one cord of four-foot wood from it in thirty-eight minutes, the record number of cubic feet contained in a stick of board timber cut

Max O. Lee

Depot, Soo Junction.

north of town, and above all, praise for its celery gardens and its blast furnace. Regular features were "Dollarville Doings" and "Deer Park Drift." It was a time of intensely personal journalism, and the utmost frankness and candor seemed to be the order of the day. When a man or an enterprise suited the editor he openly wished him or it well in his weekly columns, and when he was against something or somebody, he openly said so. From time to time he found it necessary to lambast a rival editor or to reply to one's deprecatory remarks.

In 1899 the paper was acquired by William G. Fretz, who had taken employment there twelve years earlier. A staunch supporter of the community, he was editor and publisher for fifty years, and was recognized at the time of his death in 1949 as the dean of Upper Peninsula newspapermen. The editorship and journalistic traditions then passed to his son, Merle B. Fretz, whose work with the paper had begun in 1919. In 1971 Merle's son and associate, William M. Fretz, took up the reins.

In its first issue the *News* reported that W.O. Strong, land commissioner for the railroad company, was overseeing an agricultural venture:

... Along the line of the D. M. & M. railroad on the eastern confines of the town, the company has cleared, stumped and fenced about 2 1/2 acres of land, the surface soil of which consists of black muck, 7 feet deep ... on which C. McFarlane, the company's professional gardener, is putting celery plants [38,000] which were raised in hot beds near the Newberry Hotel.

John G. Van Tuyl came from the Grand Rapids area to manage the successful enterprise, and after a year or so began his own farm, the O. K. Celery Gardens, now a truck farm run by his grandson and known as Lone's Gardens.

Though once widely known as "Celery City," Newberry's role as an agricultural center (never large) peaked out about 1920. Farming was concentrated, for soil reasons, along the southern edge of the Tahquamenon waterway, and, more importantly, in the Manistique Lakes region of Luce County. According to 1890 census figures, there were 55 farms in the county. The three most important crops (in order of acreage allotted to them) were hay, oats and potatoes.

Nevertheless, there were often high hopes expressed that some innovation would prove to be a real money-maker, a bonanza to the farmer. As one writer, Dr. George F. Deasy, put it in an article in 1950: "Celery, sheep, beef cattle, peas, swine, orchards, barley, sunflowers, rye, wheat, corn, alfalfa and fur farming all were hopefully tried, but without success." And the dream of a stockyard also came and went.

Without success were the recurrent schemes to drain thousands of acres of Tahquamenon lowland for agriculture. The pine lands north of the river simply were not suited to farming, although those concerned with the disposal of cutover lands actively encouraged such settlement.

The population of Newberry, compared with that of most communities in southeastern Michigan, has grown very slowly. It was put at 2,465 in 1930; and at only 2,300 in 1970, when the census showed a population of 6,700 in the entire county. In 1890 half of the county's 2,400 persons had been born outside the United States, chiefly in Scandinavia and Canada.

Two factors ensured a certain stability underlying the slow growth of the community. One was the variety of wood species available for lumbering. Of perhaps greater importance over the long pull was the establishment of a state mental hospital, built just south of the village in 1895. Newberry had been one of seven Upper Michigan towns invited to offer sites. The proposal of the local committee took up nearly half the pages of a pamphlet devoted to all seven presentations. In addition to getting down to the basic offer of free land, and the cost of wells and a pumping plant, it covered geology, climate, epidemics, prevailing winds, temperature and moisture of the air. It spoke of infrequency of cold local rains, praised the mellow winds of Lake Superior, and when it came to the Tahquamenon, pointed out that the banks are "largely drift-lined and high, with many outcroppings and glittering quartz."

As planned originally, there were to be twenty buildings placed in the form of a quadrangle and connected by covered porches, with a capacity of 985 patients. The first cost of maintaining patients was reckoned at 50 cents a day; attendants' pay ranged from $16 to $26 a month. The institution was enlarged over the years, and, with as many as 600 local residents employed there, once provided the principal single payroll of the community.

In 1960 the mentally ill division housed 1,436. In addition about 400 patients were accommodated in a cluster of buildings known as the Children's Unit, which was built in 1941. Great progress has been made, especially in the past decade or two, in the treatment of mental illness; and, as a consequence, hospital stays are on the average much shorter than formerly. Emphasis has now been put on establishing as many patients as possible in home environments. As a result, the hospital population and employees have been greatly reduced.

Geographical location also played a part in the eventual location at Newberry of regional headquarters of other state

R.A. Brotherton

Tug "Betty B" tows barge on Tahquamenon River trip, c. 1930.

Toonerville Trolley, 1928.

agencies: State Police, Department of Natural Resources, and Department of State Highways and Transportation. In 1937, when the state bought from the Cleveland-Cliffs Iron Company the land (an uncut hardwood forest) surrounding the Upper Falls, it assured the creation of the Tahquamenon Falls State Park. This fulfilled years of hopes and plans on the part of various conservation groups. One of the prime movers was Newberry's Joseph P. Rahilly, for many years member and chairman of the Michigan Conservation Commission. Now encompassing the two waterfalls and extensive campgrounds, the park is a great tourist attraction. Popular river trips to the Upper Falls still take off from Beach's boat landing and from Slater's landing.

Thus Newberry withstood the loss created by the removal of old-growth timber hereabout and did not suffer the decline seen in many towns dependent solely upon lumber or mining. Sawmills are still in operation here, and timber harvesting, which began in earnest over a century ago, is still very much a factor in community life.

In the autumn of 1882 dynamite boomed near the Upper Falls. A section of rock-bed in the rapids was blasted out in an attempt (only partially successful) to improve drainage of the great lowland upstream and facilitate log driving. (In the spring of 1923, water completely flooded the rails in the Sage Swamp near Soo Junction. J.B. Crowley, a veteran crew member between the Junction and the Sault, told me, "The water got as high as two feet over the rails and we had to carry wood on the back

J.B. Crowley

DSS&A passenger train crossing Sage Swamp west of Soo Junction, 1923.

of the tank to light a new fire in the boiler after we got through the water. The section crew patrolled the right of way in a rowboat to push the logs and old ties off the track.")

The theater of operations was ready; the lines of assault formed quickly. As was the case with many of the large stands of pine in the Upper Peninsula, the men and companies who were largely responsible for its removal were those who had lumbered extensively in the river basins of the Lower Peninsula - the Muskegon, Manistee, Saginaw, Au Sable - and moved north to tackle other pineries.

With the building of the big steam sawmills, the pace of life quickened. Men's destinies, once linked simply to the hewing of axes and the meeting of waters, became tied even more closely to the meshing of gears. Behind the ponderous efficiency of the big steam mills there was an array of sights and sounds that could keep old men absorbed and young boys virtually goggle-eyed - the soft but compelling hiss of escaping steam at the carriage that bore the log into the main saw - the persistent clamor of the gang saws, working up and down upon squared cants with a precise and relentless exaction, until, as an old-time lumber grader described, it seemed literally to "rain lumber" on the endless chain transporting the boards away.

Dollarville

At the time Newberry was being established, Robert Dollar, later to gain fame in West Coast shipping, located the American Lumber Company's mill a mile west on the railroad, thus building in 1882 the first major mill on the Tahquamenon and founding Dollarville.

He sold the mill after only five years, presumably to the Peninsular Land & Manufacturing Company, whose ownership was interlocked with that of the DM&M Railroad Company. The mill then went to the Dollarville Lumber Company in 1892 in what was probably a reorganization move. A firm that had already lumbered in the Ludington area for over twenty years, Danaher & Melendy, took over in 1895 and ran until the pine cut was finished in 1903. Other species were sawed into the 1920's. About the time of World War I, the South Shore Cedar Company was operating a line to bring in logs from the area. Dollarville is now a site for the decking and loading of pulpwood and of a flooding project for fish and wildlife propagation.

One hundred bushels of potatoes is said to have been the payment for the first lumber sawed at Dollarville. It went to build a barn on the homestead of Robert Bryers, who in 1877 was one of the first to settle in the Manistique Lakes area. He had known Dollar years earlier in Bracebridge, Ontario.

Dollar, who emigrated to Canada from Scotland in 1858, moved to Michigan in July 1882, making headquarters at Marquette, where, he had said, he "got out fine large timber for the English market." He built the mill near Newberry to manufacture lumber from the logs that were not suitable for the square-hewn timber demanded by the foreign trade. During his relatively few years in Michigan he sent eight or ten shiploads to England, besides ten to fifteen million feet of logs to the mill to be sawed.

In his memoirs he wrote: "While I was looking up a mill site, as well as timber for the mill at Dollarville, the railroad was under course of construction at this point. It was a wild, undeveloped country. . . . With a man to help me I went to the end of the railroad." Although they had camping gear, it was a bitterly cold January night, and they were persuaded to stay with one O'Brien and his wife, who kept a camp for about twenty-five construction workers. It was a decision to regret. There was a big brawl that night caused by a barrel of whiskey, which Mrs. O'Brien had "strengthened," or increased the amount in the barrel by adding water, pepper and blue-stone (copper sulphate). A lamp was knocked over, the "shanty" caught fire, and Dollar awakened to join the others in saving it.

He also wrote of the observance of July 4, 1883:

> It being the first national holiday for the village, we had a celebration. The men got filled up with bad whiskey and there was, of course, a free-for-all fight. Two of the worst fellows were arrested. But there was no lock-up so the Justice of the Peace came to me to know what to do with them. I saw a box car on the siding so I said, "put them in it and lock the door." The next morning the Justice reported that a freight train had taken that car to Marquette, one hundred miles distant. The fellows woke up the next morning when a brakeman opened the door. On learning where they were, they took to their heels and disappeared in the town, so we had a good riddance.

Dollar said that in Michigan he found there were large tracts of government land for sale at $1.25 an acre. "I invested every cent I had in this land and it proved to be a good investment." After the Dollars moved to California in 1888, it took three or four years to close out the Michigan business and sell the land, which amounted to over 20,000 acres. Winter trips to warmer climates had led to the choice of San Francisco as a place to settle. There he continued in lumbering and invested in ocean-going vessels.

The pine country northwest of Dollarville fed logs to the local mill. In 1891 the Peninsular Lumber & Manufacturing Company was operating five camps with a total of about 250 men. By December it already had 11 million feet of logs on skidways in the woods. Wages throughout the period averaged about a dollar a day for most men. Michigan enacted a ten-hour day law for sawmills in 1885, and it is likely that most of the Dollarville lumber was produced on this basis. The company had an insurance plan for its men that was unusual for the time - long before enactment of the Workmen's Compensation Act. It deducted fifty cents per month from their wages and guaranteed

Giant birch burl used as flagpole base in Dollarville, c. 1890's.

them medical attention, board and $13 per month if laid up because of accident. Although the benefits may seem incredibly small by today's standards, the plan was a pioneering one in the region at that time.

In January 1892, forty loaded cars were arriving daily by logging railroad. Logs were also brought by river driving, but, especially after 1895, railroading appears to have been favored. The Tahquamenon above Dollarville was not the easiest stream to drive logs on, partly because of weeds in some of its shallows.

After the Danaher & Melendy purchase, C.D. (Con) Danaher managed the mill and lived at Newberry, where he built a large frame home with quarters for the servants and a third-floor classroom for his children. In the 1890's improvements were made in the plant to increase its capacity and efficiency: a band saw on one side of the mill to reduce wastage in sawing, and a

Marquette County Historical Society

Log landing and mill, Dollarville.

dynamo for the generation of electricity to permit lighting up
the place to run at night. The average daily cut at the mill was
100,000 board feet. Their advertisement in *The Newberry News*
boasted: "The market where everything from a toothpick to a
piece of waney board timber is bought for cash and sold on the
same basis." One rather unusual feature of the Dollarville
operations was that, unlike nearly all other large lumber shipping
centers in the Upper Peninsula, owners had to rely on rail
shipment of all of their products.

In November 1896 the Dollarville correspondent to the
Newberry paper reported: "C. Chamberlain, lumber inspector,
and Jerry the tally boy are in town this week." The job of a tally
boy in those days was to mark down footage and grade notations
as the lumber inspector, moving across the piles of pine with his
scaling stick, called them out. "Jerry the tally boy" was Jerry L.
Lynch, who became a trusted lumber inspector at the big mills
and a prominent lumberman in eastern Upper Michigan.

About the time they finished cutting their pine, Danaher told
R.C. Hulbert, a timber cruiser at that time, that the firm wondered
whether its cutover lands were worth paying taxes on. He asked
Hulbert to run through them and give him an opinion. Hulbert
said that some of the lands were worthless but some had low
grade hardwood on them suitable for making charcoal. "Charcoal
iron was in demand, and I had reason to believe that the
Cleveland-Cliffs Iron Company would buy the lands. On a three-
percent commission basis, I took the matter up with their land

agent. I sold for over fifty thousand dollars the lands the Danahers thought might not be worth the payment of taxes."

The Newberry News of April 1, 1921, announced the untimely death of Danaher at age sixty-four:

"At the End of the Rope," was the metaphorical message that Cornelius D. Danaher, Tacoma millionaire lumberman ... left for his friends, the public and the world to solve, before taking his life by hanging himself from a piling of the Danaher Lumber Company's mill dock near Tacoma, Washington. His body was discovered floating in the bay on March 17.

Emerson

Three other principal millsites, Emerson, Deer Park and Shelldrake, all on the shore of Lake Superior, joined Dollarville in the encirclement of Tahquamenon pine.

To the Tahquamenon by schooner came the mill of Alonzo Chesbrough, who was moving north from Bay City and Toledo. With two purchases - the second completed in 1880 - he had acquired in excess of 30,000 acres of carefully selected pine land. His mill, built at the mouth of the river, burned down within a year or two. Experience with storms rolling in off Lake Superior indicated the need for a more protected site, and the new location was chosen a few miles south at Emerson, named for Chesbrough's fellow lumberman Curtis Emerson of Saginaw. A post office opened on April 15, 1884. The mill continued operations during the season of navigation until 1913.

It was to become the closest to a lumbering dynasty ever on the river, for the enterprise Chesbrough founded was carried on after his death in 1887 by his sons, Abraham, Frank, Fremont and Aaron. Abraham (A.M.) handled the selling, Frank the woods, Fremont (Free) the mill, and Aaron, who spent less time at Emerson than the others, the Toledo office.

The firm dominated in pine logging, river driving and lumber shipments on the eastern half of the watershed, and its operation was financially profitable. During the nearly thirty years of the cut, the price of pine lumber rose to a high of $35 per thousand board feet. Their costs probably did not exceed twelve dollars. They dredged from deep water in the bay to their docks to permit

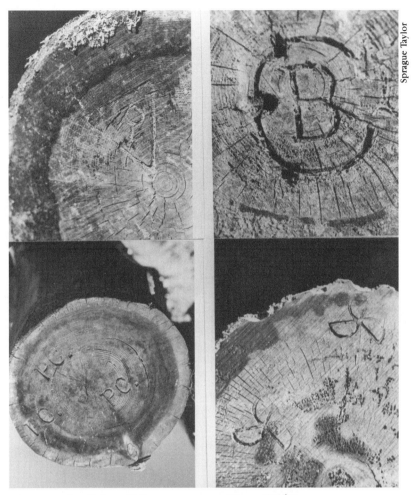

Sprague Taylor

Log marks from Tahquamenon Bay, 1947.

boat loading, and from the river to their mill boom to provide for direct running of their logs to the mill. By dredging they also cut off the wide bend just upstream from the mouth. In 1886 they organized the Tahquamenon Boom Company which under state license sorted logs and herded them into boom pockets at the mouth of the river, each owner's separated according to a stamped mark.

The Chesbroughs had their own lumber carrier, the steam freighter *Peshtigo*, and also a tug, the *George Rogers*, often used to tow rafts of logs bought along the Lake Superior shore. George (Cap) Rogers was in charge of the booms and sorting gap and also

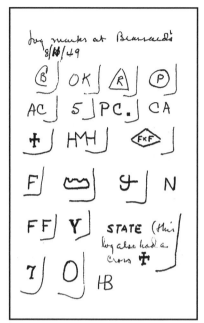

Author's sketch of log marks, 1949.

of the tug that bore his name. He had been a great friend of Alonzo and came to Emerson as captain of the original tug, the *Josephine*. With him was William Wallace, who later ran the store, as the mate.

W.J. Chesbrough, Frank's son, spent vacations during his teen years at Emerson. Reminiscing in 1947, he recalled "Cap" as "a tall, lean, leathery cuss. He looked like a lumberjack, with his trousers rolled up to the top of his high boots and an open woolen shirt. He had a cud of tobacco in his cheek, continually. I really think he held it there so constantly his cheek formed this little bulge and it became permanent." He was an excellent sailor. The Chesbroughs had one or two barges, and the *Rogers* towed them out into the lake, loaded, then gave them over to the *Peshtigo* to be towed down East with lumber. The *Rogers* also went to the Sault for supplies and frequently towed barges up from below for lumber.

The owners and employees came and went by boat; natives were often brought over from the community at Bay Mills to load lumber. When the Chesbroughs needed an outlet that could be used in the winter when the boats were laid up, they built a road over twenty miles long, bridging both the East Branch of the Tah-quamenon and the Hendrie River. It ran from Emerson to a point on the railroad then called the Black Cut, later called Peshims, where the railroad now intersects highway M-28. If deep snow made the trip more than a day, one could stay at a cabin built as a halfway house along the way. After the railroad from Soo Junction to the Sault was built, the Chesbroughs abandoned the Black Cut road and built a road between Emerson and Eckerman, where a station had been established with an agent, a post office and a telegraph office. Later a part of highway M-123,

W.J. Chesbrough

Tug "Josephine" at Emerson dock, c. 1900. Fremont Chesbrough, center.

its sixteen miles were grubbed out of the forest in the fall of 1891, according to *The Newberry News*, by Solon Lester and a gang of twenty men he brought from Newberry. Corduroy, a kind of pavement of poles, was put down on the road which connected with one that ran from Emerson north to Whitefish Point. It acquired the name the Wire Road from the telegraph wire that followed along it to the Coast Guard station at the Point.

The mill at Emerson was equipped with two band saws and a small gang saw, and powered by three steam engines. Its capacity was 100,000 to 125,000 board feet per day. Because Chesbrough timber contained a large percentage of big trees, they produced better than the average run of lumber by grade. Large amounts of "deal" timber - choice, clear timber - were shipped. Much of the product went to Tonawanda, New York, and to Chicago. Jerry Lynch was the shipping inspector for many years.

The big steam mills constructed their company towns. At Emerson there were about thirty houses, and a particularly well-stocked company store, described by W.J. Chesbrough from personal recollection:

> Owing to Emerson being almost completely isolated from outside - depending for its supplies on a sixteen-mile road through the hardwood or on boats which came up about once every two weeks, this store had to carry everything the populace desired, from salt pork to sewing needles.

Wooden shelves high up to the ceiling on three sides; wooden counters with the big cheeses on one end; barrels of crackers, pretzels, sour pickles, salt pork, flour, etc., flanking the fronts of them. The old wood-burning stove stood in the center of the floor on a big square of sheet iron, spittoons at the four corners of this, and wooden chairs all around. In one corner was the "Post Office" and in another the apothecary shop; at the front was a showcase with its corn-cob pipes and Battle Axe Plug, Honey Chew, Sweet Burley, etc.; another case held the stick candy, horehound and peanut brittle. Farther down were tables of dress goods and calicos for the women and corduroy pants and woolen shirts for the men. Old Bill Wallace, a Civil War sailor, ran the store. He disbursed groceries, tobacco, candy and dress goods all day long. He even helped the women make up their dresses from his goods, to the scorn of the teamsters and some of the woodsmen who played cards with him almost every night. He bossed the store with a heavy hand and if a woodsman got too boisterous would throw him out, bodily. He couldn't have licked any of them but he dominated them all, just the same, by his superior and fierce manner.

Other important fixtures of the mill towns were the boarding house, the blacksmith shop, the school and the company office. W.J. Chesbrough recalled Adam McIntosh, a fiery red-headed

W.D. Hulbert

Wanigan and boom, 1904.

Scotchman who kept the books at Emerson, standing up at a long high desk to make the entries:

Mac kept all the books, ledger, journal, day book, etc., in longhand and it was beautiful copy. He wore a pair of thick-lensed glasses and a green eye-shade, through which his red hair stuck up at a sharp angle, and he always looked under the glasses while copying, tilting his chin up in order to do so. He kept a "copy" in his head, and many times answered questions as to figures and boat loading detail in considerable volume without once going to the books for information. On Sundays he put on an old frock coat, and, whenever there was no traveling minister present, he preached the sermon and led the choir. He never wore but one suit (so far as I could tell), a dead black one, coat high cut on lapels, square cut at bottom, very shiny at the elbows, very baggy at the knees and the whole thing set off by an enormous gold watch chain, like a logging chain, running from one pocket to the other in a very shiny vest. His watch was a heavy thick gold one wound up by a key. He performed this winding operation each morning upon entering the office, but would forget it about two days out of the week, to his eternal disgust.

The Chesbrough brothers went their separate ways in 1912, with "Free" remaining to finish at Emerson and Frank starting a mill at Wilwin near Trout Lake, an operation which ran steadily until 1922, intermittently thereafter, and was gone by 1929 - as were most of the others of the epoch of pine.

W.D. Hulbert

At the brink of the Upper Falls, 1904.

Charles Beaulieu

Stage transportation, 1890's.

Deer Park

Thirty miles north of Newberry on the shore of Lake Superior was the site of the Deer Park Life Saving Station. One of the first on the lake, it was established in 1876. Among others commissioned along the shore at the same time were those at the mouth of the Two Hearted River, at Crisp Point and at Vermilion Point. The Whitefish Point Lighthouse had been established in 1847.

Lumbering at Deer Park began in earnest with the construction of the Cook & Wilson mill in 1887. It was built on the north bank of Muskallonge Lake, which was separated from Lake Superior (over thirty feet lower) by a narrow neck of land. Lumber docks were put on Lake Superior and all shipments out were by vessel.

By midsummer of 1888 the mill was set up to saw 160,000 board feet every twenty-four hours, night running being made possible by the recent innovation of the electric light. The population was nearing three hundred. The settlement could be reached by a crude road from Newberry. Soon it was served by a school, a post office (an old photograph shows them combined in one building), and the horse-drawn stage of William Green, who also ran the only hotel. In winter storms, Dan McLeod's dogs, Grover and Cleveland, were sometimes put into harness to carry the mail up from Newberry.

By 1891 the mill had been taken over by Bradley & Hurst, who

Matt Surrell

Lumber schooner, *"Huron City"*, with a load of lumber from Cook & Wilson, Deer Park, c. 1890.

ran it night and day that spring. Railroad logging was being done for them by the firm of Mutart & O'Malley, who delivered over 17 million feet that summer and fall to the millsite. There the logs were dumped from a trestle running into a bay of the lake, forming a handy logpond.

The cut was ended about 1900; the equipment was taken out, and Bradley moved west to Oregon. Sam McTiver purchased the old log mark rights and in 1912 brought in a portable mill and proceeded to salvage the logs that had sunk to the bottom of Muskallonge Lake during the course of the years. From the old dock on Lake Superior he shipped over half a million board feet of lumber gained from those logs.

In October 1903, *The Newberry News* informed its readers that Sheriff Cyr had left for Chicago to be a witness in the case of the "Deer Park Swindlers." Over a year earlier, two Chicagoans, under the name of Deer Park Improvement Association, had bought a tract of cut-over land from Bradley & Hurst, platted it into town lots, and issued a glowing prospectus. This was, said the *News*, "a neatly printed folder, containing illustrations of churches, school houses, manufactures, fine dwellings and business blocks along paved streets, a government pier, sailing and freight vessels." A two-page map gave a view of a thriving "Deer Park."

A check of the original plat shows over eighty blocks, with

J.V. Kinsey

Alta Lodner and Deer Park school (sign reads "Post Office").

eighty 25 x 125 foot lots to a block, wide streets and avenues, among them Grand Avenue, Oakwood Boulevard, and Indiana Avenue. The owners were alleged to have secured thousands of dollars from small investors who had, in reality, bought a few feet of sand plains. A surveyor told the grand jury that the only life he saw - vegetable or animal - was a cloud of sand flies, the only building a fisherman's empty hut. The taxes in 1902 on the entire acreage had amounted to seventy-three cents!

Shelldrake

Milling operations at the mouth of the Shelldrake (Betsy) River on Whitefish Bay were begun by the Penoyer brothers of Bay City with the construction of their mill in 1895. They owned a large block of pine lands west of Shelldrake and extending south close to the Tahquamenon River below the falls. The copper mining company, Calumet & Hecla, bought the mill and uncut timber in 1899, continuing the contract with Con Culhane for

Jennie House

Moore, Park and Sharp steamhauler, Shelldrake, 1904.

railroading the logs. They shipped large quantities of mine timbers for their mines.

A young woman schoolteacher, Carrie Sprague, roomed with the family of the mill superintendent. She was my aunt. Writing of that time, she said, "The board here was of the best the place afforded, and I paid accordingly. While teachers' wages in upper Michigan were but $27.00 [per month], board was about $10.00. I used to don a swimming costume and jacket and go for a swim on fine mornings before the workmen were awake. [It has always seemed to me that anyone who made a practice of taking morning dips in Whitefish Bay must have some inner strength and fortitude.] I passed the home of a bird dog, and he would follow me into the water, which was so cold we did not play about in it but a few minutes."

Shelldrake had a relatively long life as a lumbering village. Calumet & Hecla sold out to Bartlett Bros., a Canadian firm, about 1910, and railroading to the mill continued, using Culhane's two engines, until the plant burned (for the second time) in 1925. (Because the Bartlett operation seemed plagued by accidents, some employees thought it was "marked" for trouble. Frank Warner told about the time the boiler in the machine shop blew up, killing two of the men. This happened one morning about 8:00 a.m. Warner was working on one of the elevated tramways nearby, and he remembered hearing the rivets being sheared like the sound of a .22 rifle, just before the blast took

C.L. Scott

The "Nipissing" of the Bartlett Lumber Company, Shelldrake.

place. One of the men was not killed outright and had to be removed from the debris and taken to the hospital which was in the back of the men's camp. The engineer, Hank Murphy, was then dispatched with his switch engine, the "3-spot," to get the doctor, who at the time was fishing up the grade at Sweeney Creek, and Warner pictured quite vividly going up and down the hills with the throttle tied down. Once a sawyer was caught while installing new machinery; and another time it was three Swedes in charge of sandholes up the grade who were buried alive when they dug too far into the side of a bank.) After the fire of 1916, a mill was brought up from Deward, scene of the cutting of the last timber owned by David Ward, a Michigan pine king. This mill was said by its builders to be the finest in the world at the time it was constructed. Two sets of timber, 14 inches x 14 inches, cut from clear white pine 54 feet long, supported its width; in length it was 307 feet. It employed one band and one circular saw, and turned out about 77,000 feet a day, in contrast to the 130,000 the Penoyer mill had been capable of sawing.

When the Bartletts first came to Shelldrake, they took out a considerable amount of waney board timber and loaded it on vessels off the tramway that had been constructed there earlier by the Penoyer brothers. According to Jerry Lynch, the boat they loaded for a Canadian concern in 1913 was the last shipped out.

C.L. Scott

Fourth of July log birling, Shelldrake.

Grass grew on the millsites and the long docks crumbled. But they hung on a long time - Shelldrake until 1925. Fire, the eternal nemesis of sawdust towns, took the mill, that heavily constructed mill whose proud makers boasted would be the finest in the world.

By no means all of the pine cut on the watershed went to the four original mills. Much of it was towed in rafts to the Hall and Munson operation at Bay Mills and more was sawed in Sault Ste. Marie. By the turn of the century, Hall and Munson had put up two sawmills, plus a box factory and a sash and door factory at Bay Mills. The beautiful steam yacht of the elegant Mr. Hall was often seen tied up at the mill dock. One of their chief suppliers was Frank Perry, who had started logging here in the board timber era. Later, as pine was harder to get, he turned his attention to pulpwood, towing most of the wood to Green Bay where it was sold to adjacent paper mills.

Although the Two Hearted River region had no large pine mills, it was the scene of extensive cutting. Here Con Culhane jobbed with his logging railroad for John Torrent, prominent Muskegon lumberman, who, with Patrick A. Ducey, put up a mill at the Sault in the Algonquin area, in 1891.

Other, smaller, mills came and went, with profitable runs of varying lengths of time. John and Robert Hunter of Newberry put in a mill on the mainstream about 1910, and operated a railroad line connecting it with the DSS&A at Soo Junction. The

Russell Goodeman

Bartlett mill, Shelldrake, burning in 1916.

Toonerville Trolley, a narrow gauge carrying tourists to excursion boats at the site of Hunter's Mill, follows this grade.

The Cadillac-Soo Lumber Company built a mill in the Sault and commenced logging operations in the eastern portion of the Tahquamenon region in 1923, as a result of the consolidation of timber holdings of Cadillac Lumber & Chemical Company, Richardson Avery Company, and Raco Land & Timber Company. Several lines were used for railroad logging, totaling possibly two hundred miles of grade, and there were as many as fifteen camps at one time. Bob LaRock was the "walking boss" for many years.

At Eckerman in 1924 the E.H. Sheldon Company of Muskegon established a mill adjacent to the DSS&A. It operated a logging railroad into its holdings for about ten years; the mill ran off and on for about thirty-five years.

It was when the big stands of pine had largely vanished in the Tahquamenon country that the equally large stands of hardwood and short stuff - as pulpwood and cedar products are commonly called - came into their own. Up and down the railroad between Trout Lake and McMillan and between Soo Junction and Strongs, the banking grounds and spurs of these operators came into being. Some of the pine men stayed. Many went on over into Wisconsin and Minnesota. [I am told that when A.M. Chesbrough was asked why more of them did not stay behind, he replied without hesitation, "The romance went out of it," and probably to a very great extent this is true.] If peaveys, cork boots and stagged pants may be said to have been the hallmarks of the men in the day of pine, perhaps it may likewise be said that tarpaper, haywire, and Peerless contributed in no small measure to the efforts of those whose work it was to take pulpwood, ties and fence posts from a dozen different stretches of inhospitable muck-swamp.

Although pine predominated in the cutting of the early years, the country was unusual in that it contained a considerable amount of other marketable species within its approximately 800 square miles. In fact the harvesting of them continues. Geological happenstance, with its formation of streamside swamps coupled with highlands of hardwoods, made for a diversified forest, and so it has been that the removal of timber such as hardwoods, jackpine, and second-growth pulpwood remains fairly constant. In this respect the valley has been spared the pine barren appearance of some other regions. Literally thousands of men have been employed at one time or another in the cutting of pulpwood for the making of paper. Others, also unnumbered - in an industry that began almost coincidentally with the major episode of pine - were occupied in its swamps with hewing cedar ties for railroads, making cedar posts for farms all across the midwest, and for turning the cedar butt logs into shingles. Taken as a whole, the industry has known its ups and downs of prosperity, a low period being the Panic of 1893, and again, and most seriously, the Great Depression of the 1930's.

Notwithstanding these setbacks, it has continued and remains a major economic factor of the area today. If the major day of pine and its colorful lumberjacks is gone, the steady hum of saws, powered now and not dragged by hand, still creates islands of sound across much of the Tahquamenon Valley.

Copied from the version tacked up at the Sheldon Mill. Author unknown.

Saw Mill for Sale

One hay-wire sawmill,
  Nice new location,
Ten mile haul,
  To the shipping station.
Half mile to plank road,
  Rest of it mud,
Six bridges, all condemned
  But otherwise good.
Timber shaky hemlock,
  Very few knots,
Awfully sound
  Between rotten spots.
Fire box boiler,
  Flues leak some,
Injector patched
  With chewin' gum.
Darn good whistle
  And carriage track,
Nine feet left
  Of old smoke stack.

Belts a little ragged,
  Rats ate the laces,
Head saw cracked
  In a couple of places.
The engine knocks
  And is loose on its base,
And the fly wheel's broke
  In just one place.
There's a pile of old lumber
  And a few cull ties,
But they've been attached
  By some creditor guys.
There's a mortgage on the land
  That's now past due,
And I still owe
  For the machinery, too.
But if you want to get rich
  Here's the place to begin,
For it's a darn good layout
  For the shape it's in.

The Saga of Con Culhane

One day in the summer of 1893 *The Newberry News* announced that a new logger had appeared on the Lake Superior shore about thirty-five miles north of town. A visitor to his headquarters described the work done there since the previous fall as "something incredible." There were camps for two hundred men. A railroad, an innovation in these woods, was being thrust south. Down the standard gauge track a huffing little engine, its whistle and bell busy, was pulling loaded Russel (logging) cars to the landing. It appeared, the paper concluded, that this newcomer understood his business.

It has required the work of many to take the measure of Tahquamenon trees. Indeed, the cutting continues and probably will indefinitely. But here was one who not only typified an era, but who left a singular imprint of his own on the past. As long as the years of pine are relived and retold along the river, men will see his bulky shadow cast, and repeat the exploits of Cornelius Culhane.

Decades have passed since the tragedy occurred that struck him down. Yet the magic of the name, entwined in myth and adorned with hearsay in the custom lumberjacks have followed the country over - the magic lingers. I have talked with a few who once knew him. Animation will grip them still as they picture him, glowering at a job-hunter with his question, "Can you fight?" or as they try to copy a rich County Cork brogue that turned "my" to "me," made of "boy" a "bye" and of "marsh" a "mayrsh." Best, it may be, they remember the Con Culhane, stub of cigar busy, hands hooked in suspenders at his stocky chest, who would nod at his smaller locomotive, the *Ellen K.*, and marvel: "She's neither sleigh nor wagon; she's 'Ma's Machine!' "

A year after its first announcement, the *News* informed its readers, "Con Culhane ... was in ... purchasing supplies. He is cutting pine at the rate of about 1,000,000 feet per week." The following fall, in 1895, it reported more fully on "A Big Lumber Contract."

Proudly Culhane displayed his outfit to the visitor. Largely unlettered, he was never one to shrink from the attention of anyone who wielded pen or type. Across Little Lake (shown on some maps as Temple Lake) a brown lid of logs lay ready for rafting. For three seasons he had averaged an output of twenty million feet. Here were his crew's quarters, his blacksmith shop, his barns and storehouses and carpenter shop; over there was his home, identified wherever he lived in the North as the "White House."

Obviously impressed with the big logger's hospitality, the reporter joined Culhane and his "amiable lady" for dinner, to find a table set like that in a "first class hotel."

He had blazed a long trail from Port Austin, the little town in the Michigan Thumb district he called home. Born in Ireland in 1847, a youthful immigrant who lost his mother on the long Atlantic voyage, he settled, in the tradition of his forebears, on the land. There had been a little Huron County farm and hard scrabbling. There had been a fire, it was said, that wiped out meager possessions. As he consoled his young wife - the warm-hearted Ellen Kennedy who had joined him from Canada - he promised that one day they would ride in their own handsome

Mrs. August Gottschalk

Mrs. August Gottschalk

Cornelius Culhane. **Ellen Culhane.**

carriage. It would have windows up front on both sides, he assured her.

At twenty-five he was logging in a small way along the Muskegon River. With the staunch companionship of this woman who was to live in the devoted, respectful memories of a small army of woodsmen as "Ma" Culhane, his status grew. Not a buyer of timber himself, he buckled down to showing its owners how to move it.

Preceding his railroading venture was a busy period of nearly twenty years of sleigh-haul logging. One of his former employees, James Ahearn of Kinde, wrote in 1945 about being with Culhane at Higgins Lake sixty years earlier: "The crew at that time numbered about 100. We all did a lot of hard work for him. Sixteen hours was considered a work day, and $1.00 per day was tops."

At times Con and Ellen rode behind a smart pair of drivers, "Pacer Prince" and "Mabel Wood." Once his wife persuaded him to stay long enough in Bay City to be photographed in broadcloth and stand-up collar. As successes were tallied up, he saw that she owned befitting finery.

His last Lower Michigan logging was done in Newaygo County in 1891-1892. John Torrent, the Muskegon lumberman who was reputed to have sold a billion feet of boards in his day, had just bought a big tract along the Little Two Hearted River for the firm of Torrent & Ducey. He proposed to build a mill at the Sault. Would Culhane take off the timber? He would indeed.

Now as he entered the fall of 1895, his Lake Superior beachhead was marked by three years of action. Many of his capable hands from the "Berrypatch," as they called the home grounds of Port Austin, were still with him. He had a logger's good show. Most of the Little Two Hearted terrain was level, the timber thick. Little Lake provided a natural log pond of over a hundred acres, sheltered by a narrow spit of land from storms on Lake Superior. He had built a connecting sluiceway. Shut off, it provided a haven. Opened in good rafting weather, it made a convenient funnel through which logs flowed, two million feet or so at a time, into the confines of awaiting boomsticks for towing downlake.

Only that spring the *Grand Rapids Democrat* had paid him more than dutiful notice:

C. Culhane ... , the "king logger" of the northwest, was here today negotiating with lumberman John Torrent... . The history of Culhane's career in the forests of Michigan begins with the lumber industries of Muskegon and it is estimated that the logs, the movement of which he has superintended from the woods to streams and railroads, would constitute a forest of 2,000 square miles.

If favorable logging conditions helped Culhane make a stake, they did not do the same for his employer. Heavily mixed through the Little Two Hearted stand was red pine, and sales for it were sometimes slow. Before the close of the operation, there were attachments for nonpayment of taxes. The "Cleveland Panic," though short-lived, hit hard. Tersely, *The Newberry News* had explained the lumberman's plight in September 1893: "The Torrent mill at the Soo has been shut down for want of piling room for lumber for which there is no sale."

The Torrent tract exhausted, Culhane contracted with Chesbrough Brothers of Emerson to build thirty-five miles of new trackway, and to send pine from their remaining holdings into booms at the mouth of the Tahquamenon. Ingeniously taking his railroad equipment cross-country, he moved into the Chesbrough domain in 1897. In less time than might be required now to

Culhane camp in Lower Michigan. Con and Ellen in cutter.

prepare the blueprints, he bridged the Tahquamenon and shoved a grade northeast to a landing six miles below the Lower Falls. A new home, built on a flat above the river, gave the place the name it still carries, White House Landing.

Here he spent several years, laying track deeper into the Chesbrough pine. Supplies came up the river by tug, and in from Eckerman by team across his tote- trail to the Wire Road. Visitors to this busy headquarters were numerous; he and "Ma" Culhane liked to entertain relatives and friends from down below.

As the scope of his enterprise grew, he turned northward. In the fall of 1899 he contracted with Penoyer Bros. & Company to move logs to their plant at Shelldrake, the milltown on Whitefish Bay. He agreed to furnish up to forty miles of grade. His trains were to haul not less than 100,000 and not more than 200,000 feet daily. When the Penoyers sold out shortly to the giant Calumet & Hecla Mining Company, Culhane logged for the new owners. In 1892 he confided to Will Ranson that the year just ending had seen him complete his largest deliveries - thirty-four million feet. His last headquarters was to be at Shelldrake.

With his flair for work, and with able crews, a system of log movement evolved that was honed to a wire edge of efficiency.

In addition to the *Ellen K.* he had a heavier locomotive of about forty tons, the *Con C.* To their owner, reared in a tradition of horse and ox power, and pleased with the force created by "water gone crazy," they remained "Ma's Machine" or "My Machine," objects of continual display and wonderment.

Newspapers were to guess him a millionaire. After his death one even said, "According to the opinion of men who were acquainted with him, he had more ready money than any man in the state." There is little doubt that some of this exaggeration was due to Culhane himself. Considering his lack of vested interest in either tree or finished board, he had fared well. If he had not made a million, as they frankly surmised, he had apparently put a fourth of one in the barrel.

With the expansiveness of those whose beginnings lean toward simple reckoning, he associated money with barrels. If you knew him, you realized that he meant the 350-pound sugar barrels, too, and nothing smaller. When, they said, an engine jumped the track or other logging misfortune befell, he declared, "Well, we took a shovelful out of the barrel today." Or piqued by an employer, he bellowed that he had a mind to have a team and wagon hitched and go settle accounts, vowing, "It'll take four barrels to bring back what they owe us!"

A shrewd judge of men, he had a knack of keeping them. To have worked for Culhane became a mark of distinction. And so, although they gained their knowledge of him from older campmates, for over half a century some yarning lumberjacks would affirm: "Culhane? Oh, sure. Old Con .... Yessir, knew him well."

And yet they did know him - if sometimes second-hand - in the sense that timber has always made men kin. They had heard - and repeated over many a bar - stories about this Michigan logger. Awed that this name could reach so far, they told of the immigrants, incapable of speaking English, who arrived safely on the job with placards strung on their necks, and this address, prepared for them in Finland:

N. Y. City
Sault Ste. Marie
C. Culhane.

They chuckled about the veteran canthook man. He had been

with Culhane for seventeen years without drawing all his pay or going out to town, and one holiday weekend he told his boss he would like to see Newberry for a couple of days. "Well sir, old Con grabbed him by the shoulder - and of course he had a holt on him like cat's-paw in a snaggin' chain - and he said, 'Alec, I knew when I hired you, you was a jumper.' "

Secure in the standing of veterans, they relished the case of the two greenhorns looking for work. "I was there the time they struck him for a job. Con looked 'em over a little and says, 'You boys smoke cigarettes?' And one says, 'Yep.' Con didn't go for that, on account of settin' fire in the brush in the summer. He says, 'You wear belts all the time?' 'That's right.' Con shakes his head and tells 'em, 'Sorry, but I've found that lads like you always seem to be doin' one of two things - you're either rollin' a smoke or hitchin' up your pants.' "

With approving nods, they recalled Culhane saying philosophically to a man who wanted to quit, "Well, Tim, there's nothin' tied here but the horses."

A nondrinker himself, he had a rule against bringing liquor into camp. That it remained a problem to him and other operators, nevertheless, is revealed in a newspaper item of 1893, describing the scrounging of "traveling sheebens": "Whiskey by the barrel and gallon jugs ... liquor of the poorest quality, are ... finding their way among the men employed in the woods by Bradley & Hurst and C. Culhane ... ." If, most of the time, he could keep it away from the job, he could not control it in town. One reminiscence has him striding to a foreman who had arrived in camp broke and hung over after a binge. Jerking up the man's hat and revealing a pair of blackened eyes, he roared, "Sure and you could have stayed in camp, and I'd have given you worse than that for nothing!"

Many would testify that this was no idle boast. Digging beneath hints of far-fetched praise, one must conclude that the logger, in prime condition in his six-foot, 190-pound frame, was a real adversary in a tussle. Down in the rugged atmosphere of Lower Michigan pineries he had gained his reputation as one who thoroughly enjoyed a "good rassel." He knew well the lumberjack invitation to "strip yer linen," meaning drop your hat and mackinaw, and put up your fists. And all to see, in a fraternity that scorned guns or knives, who was best man. At no time in his career, apparently, was his liveliness indulged in any bitter, knock-down and drag-out encounter. If subdued by years when he reached the Tahquamenon, the spirit of his apprenticeship never flagged; and reliable authority has vouched for one revealing incident. His patience exhausted, Culhane threw an offensive visitor through a closed cookcamp door. To the astonishment of onlookers, out of the building flew door, man, hinges, door casing and all.

Examples of his prankish prowess abound, including that of a former "road monkey," who, intent on tidying up a sleigh-road, suddenly felt a massive grip on trousers and mackinaw. The next instant he was flying into a snowdrift, a shout of Gaelic laughter ringing in his ears. An old Frenchman, still built solidly as a bear in the 1950's, would describe Culhane chasing him around a stove: "Huh!" (arms outspread and dancing in a circle) "now he come for me!"

From Bert McIlhargie, who had worked for Culhane as a youth and had followed him north, came the anecdote he told me in 1946:

> Con and his wife were drivin' down to Eckerman from the White House and they met this big jack goin' in ... said he was headin' for Culhane's Camp. Con gave him directions, not tellin' him who he was. But right away he asks, "You any good?" This fella told him he figured he could do a day's work alongside anybody. "But can you fight?" says Con. "Well" (him lookin' up at Con kind of surprised), "guess I can hold my own." "We'll see," says Con. He hands Ma the lines and down out of that buggy he goes. But pretty soon it looked like he took in a little too much territory! And there's Ma, hollerin' to the stranger, "Give it to him, give it to him - he asked for it!" Con hired him right there on the spot. Afterwards I used to hear him laugh and say he didn't mind takin' a trimmin', but he hated to have Ma sit there and tell somebody to lay it onto him.

The bonds of loyalty between him and lumberjack grew strong by such accounts, often amusingly embellished by Culhane himself. Among mill owners and business friends one heard less of rambunctious ways and more of his industry and his generosity, his devotion to his wife. Mrs. Dan McLeod, wife of a Newberry lumberman contemporary of Con's, knew the

Culhanes well. "They were," she said, "the happiest couple alive."

"Con Culhane was rough and ready on the exterior," wrote Richard Hulbert in 1947, "but that was just a covering for a warm heart and a kindly disposition." He recalled a visit to the logger's headquarters six miles below the Lower Falls.

> I saw Culhane ... at the upper side of the banking ground. We met and he said, "Looks like you are going somewhere. You usually are." I was wearing my cruising clothes and had a packsack on my back. "Yes," I said, "I have some lands to look over ... west of the river. ... Thought I might catch a logging train from here ... " "No more trains today," he said; "you'll have to stay here tonight. Come over to the cook camp." I remarked that I could wait until supper time. "No," he said, "if you come to Con Culhane's camp, you have to eat plenty and often." We walked over to the cook camp.... .Two cooks were working at the other end of the building. Culhane turned to me and said, loud enough so the cooks could hear him, "Do you see those two boys over there?" I grinned. They were both big, tall fellows. "Well," said Culhane, "about every second day I have to take them out and give them a good licking." They paid no attention to what he said but set us out a fine lunch. After eating we went over to Culhane's house (the White House) for a chat. "Ma," his wife, and "Billie," his son, were visiting in Lower Michigan. The house was beautifully furnished. I stayed there overnight and in the morning after breakfast he ordered out an extra locomotive, and I went up to the other camp "special train." All of which cost me nothing. That was typical of Con Culhane.

Precisely what caused the accident near Shelldrake on June 26, 1903, has been debated. Fifty-five years later, Edward Rudd remembered the morning vividly. As a youthful cookee, he had served Culhane his breakfast. The logger was in joshing high spirits. He felt so lively, he said, he figured he would live to be a hundred.

Usually he rode one of his trains up front, one hand on the locomotive cab and the other braced on the tender. For some reason this day he was back, or had started to walk back, on the cars. *The Evening News* heard that it happened this way:

The train was running at a good rate of speed and the brakeman was uncoupling from the engine ... .Culhane was on the end of the car ... and as the engine slacked back ... to allow the brakeman to pull the pin, the car was checked suddenly, and [Culhane] pitched forward and went under the wheels.

In the evening the tug *Merrick* crept with his broken body across Whitefish Bay, to complete the first lap of the journey home.

The tributes came, the stories grew. "The best logger in Upper Michigan," said lumberman A. M. Chesbrough. Perhaps part of the appeal lay in the name. Or perhaps it was his death, cutting him down in his prime, that gave focus to memories and brought tales to flow. True, other men in America logged more. Compared with some of the later jobs in the West, his might appear small. But to Michigan's men of the woods he was their own Paul Bunyan, of robust flesh and blood.

The Woods Fraternity

In my boyhood we lived on the edge of the lowland that follows the East Branch. As you gazed across that swamp, which today remains broken by bands of marsh and poplar-covered burning, you still saw old growth white pines outlined against the hardwoods on the northern horizon. Long ago I fixed one of them in memory by its irregular top and looming height. As I roamed the valley in the years that followed, I sought out that tree at times when I fancied myself near it. But I cannot say that I ever found it, for trees, like people, are different when viewed at close hand. That is especially so, I think, when by the circumstance of the ground you stand on, you must look up.

So like that image of the past, prominent to the eye at a distance but hard to find with surety, there is a prototype of the Tahquamenon lumberjack who is essential to this fragmentary story. Irresolutely at times, confidently at others, I have watched

Tanbark Cutters for E.H. "Pinky" Hall.

for him. In the grassed-over camp bottoms, in the caulk marks left on railroad ties, in the remembrances of old men who had pried logs loose amid the noise and spray of tons of falling water, or went out to town to raise hell, as they used to say, and put a chip under it, and yes, in yellowed pages - in all of these are clues to his essential nature. Followed awhile, his roots, like those of our northern black spruce, will be seen to have spread widely and seldom gone down. And once on his trail you may be reminded of the same tree, of its wiriness and resiliency of trunk, not to mention its gum, which is tough in the chewing but flavorsome to the taste.

If "Daylight in the swamp!" was their summons to action, and salt pork to sundown their working hours, evenings still contained a little time for relaxation. Then in the ill-lit gloom of the sleeping camp before the 9:00 p.m. lights-out, they lolled on the deacon benches for a last smoke. It was natural that they would admire feats of strength, and so they vied with each other in telling of them: of the man who carried a cookstove for some twenty miles, of the blacksmith who, one-handed, could raise an anvil by the horn, yet had so sure a touch with the tempering of iron that he "could make a baby's eye if he but had the mold." The few who could lift a barrel of sugar by the chimes and walk

Lumber camp, c. 1900.

off with it had occasion to demonstrate. Sheriff Adam Loucks of Newberry gained fame of a sort; he could crush a raw potato to pulp in either hand.

Scattered in the mythic past were the "mystery camps," abandoned with all equipment left behind. There were lost locomotives, buried to their bell-muzzle stacks, reported seen in various potholes in the Tahquamenon interior, or the skeleton found with a bear trap clamped to one porcupine-chewed leg-bone. With a sympathy that barred any incredulity they listened to the tale about the teamster and his eerie find. Headed for Emerson on a moonlit night, he rounded a bend in the tote-rode, reined in his shying horses, and looked full into the sightless eyes of a frozen man, seated beneath a tree - "and, boys, his hair turned white overnight."

Exaggeration, often supplied by an old-timer with straight-faced authority, came as if by second nature. "Halfway" John McLeod told dead-pan of his boyhood swim across a little lake north of Newberry with a stove tied to his back. The shore reached, he had been scolded by his mother for losing the lids and sent back to dive for them. There was the river driver at the Upper Falls, narrowly escaping with his life near the brink, then being sent back into the maelstrom of logs to retrieve his peavey. They told of teamsters being awakened by the redoubtable logger, Norwegian Jack Ryland, at three in the morning after an almost

Robert Nelson

Sprinkler.

continuous effort of thirty-six hours to beat the spring break-up:
"The 'Wegian shook 'em an' hollered, 'What the hell d'you want
to do - get bedsores?' " They enjoyed the leg-pulling that
Newberry's John Hunter had given a city man who marveled at
the size of a pair of big logging wheels. "Yep," said Hunter drily,
"but those are just the front pair off one of our wagons - you
should see the back ones."

They took pride in the accomplishment of "Free" (Fremont
B.) Chesbrough's prize boar. Finally penned after running loose
in the woods for several seasons, he had left carcasses of bears
"all over the place." To have hobnobbed a little with one of the
big bosses was a signal event: "Free took a likin' to me, and one
night in his office in Emerson he give me a little snort out of a
special bottle. I thought, 'Free, you're bein' kinda stingy with
that, ain't you?' But now I'll tell you somethin'. The road from
there to the boom house was grubbed a good rod wide, and I
needed every foot of it!" The other stands they had worked in
improved with the passage of years: "Boys, there was a place
down on the Manistee, and as Christ lets me live" - here a brief,
penitential look up at the camp ridgepole - "you could go jumpin'
stump to stump for six miles back from the river and never hit
the ground."

F.P. Furlong

P.M. Furlong camp near Trout Lake, 1897.

They inducted greenhorns into their fraternity with horseplay and mysterious errands. They sent them to the blacksmith for crosshauls and hand-holts, to the camp clerk for such proven remedies as extract of hammer handle; and on Sundays they were apt to embark newcomers into the woods to hunt for that elusive fur-bearer, the tree-squeak.

The lumberjacks had seasonal tides of unruliness too strong to be ignored by the local press, much though it applauded propriety and played down the antics of the Bob-Tail Element of its woodland society. *The Newberry News* veered from passing notice and oblique delicacy to dignified outrage. In 1887: "The camps breaking in this vicinity makes lively times in the village." In the spring of 1890: "The village is full of woodsmen who are 'blowing their stakes' ..."; Dollarville, according to its correspondent, was "swarming with river drivers, some caulked and some getting caulked." In 1893: "Five soiled doves were brought up from the swamp and put through Justice Main's mill last Monday." In 1898: "The ... scenes of last Sunday on the public streets, allowed to transpire without interference, would have been a disgrace even to a border town in the far west." And yet, as a foretoken of quieter days to come, there were such strange anomalies as this one reported in 1900: "The strains of 'Nearer My God to Thee,' sung in a deep bass voice, was the unusual sound which issued from one of our saloons Saturday night and caused many pedestrians to stop and stare in wonderment."

W.J. Chesbrough

Summer skidding with big wheels, 1907.

An inventive flair colored his slang, and much of it remained long after the heyday of pine was over. Men had titles befitting their jobs: the camp foreman - according to his status - was "straw-boss," "bull of the woods" or "push"; the superintendent over two or more camps, a "walking boss" or "walker"; a poor cook, a "gut-robber"; a clerk, an "ink-slinger"; a carpenter, a "wood butcher"; the workman who kept a sleighroad in shape, a "road monkey"; the one who worked the deep swamps, hewing ties or cutting shingle timber, was a "cedar savage"; and a sawmill hand, a domesticated cousin of the woods species, a "sawdust eater."

The plain fare served on camp tables gained its inevitable synonyms. Salt pork was "sowbelly"; tea, "swamp water"; a mixture of scorched grease, flour and water was called "hardwood gravy." Sausages, relative late-comers, were named "forty-five nineties," after a sizable rifle cartridge of the time. Prunes turned into "logging berries"; and pointing to stewed dried apples, a jack might, with macabre cheerfulness, ask to be handed the "dead men's ears."

At work a canthook was a "flip" or the "crooked steel"; a horse a "hay-burner"; a crosscut saw, a "briar"; and a scaling rule, a "swindle stick." To "barber-chair" a tree was to cause it to split when falling and leave part of the trunk attached to the stump. A hanging limb or a lodged tree-top, dangerous to work under, was by wary consent a "widow-maker." Snuff was "snoose"; bunks in their sleeping quarters, "muzzle-loaders"; and an inefficient company or logger was termed a "haywire outfit."

To leave a job voluntarily was to "bunch it." In this case the request given to the clerk was "Make 'er out," meaning prepare a time-check or pay order - a quiet adaptation of the irate French teamster's notice: "I come for my quit!"

Headed out of the woods for Newberry, Eckerman or Trout Lake, his "turkey" (a sack for personal possessions) on his back, a thirsty, loaded-for- bear lumberjack was conceded to be "stake-bound." Once there and bellied up to the bar, a tight-spender gained the unsavory name of a "Dick Smith," a character with short arms and deep pockets.

When it came to assigning nicknames, he went on a first-rate cognominal spree. Not content with memorializing a man's job, traits or appearance with "Peavey Tom," "Black Dan" or "Red Alec," he lavished more colorful ones upon fellow workers, walking bosses and employers alike: Paddy the Weasel, Pole-Road Wynn, Packsack Johnson, Eight-Day Bill, Runaway Shay, Butt-Log Jimmy, Five-Times Jenkins, Roothouse Joe. Likewise claiming the valley as their stamping ground were Norwegian Jack (known also as The 'Wegian), Halfway John, Catfish Jim, Pike-Eyed Green, Prodigal Jennison, and Roarin' Jimmy Gleason, whose distinctive urge it was to drag his mackinaw across a saloon floor and dare anybody to step on it. "Moonlight" Harry Schmidt was so called because of his reputation for working his crews long hours, and "Fightin' Jim" Robinson's brawlsome arrival in Newberry in the 1890's the paper might announce in a warning one-line notice - "James Robinson is in town."

The lumberjack mightily revered motherhood and respectable womanhood as those not accustomed to the protocol of woods (or temporarily forgetful of it) might learn:

I got off the northbound train at Soo Junction (remembered Jay Gerrie, a former "knight of the grip," a traveling salesman). Some of us walked over to Jack Johnson's place for a lunch. There was a roughly dressed, middle-aged lumberjack standing there, his packsack beside him. When a group of four or five women passed him, he stepped aside and took off his hat. A couple of young men, just off the same train, were standing there, and I couldn't help noticing that they seemed to kind of snicker at him for this. Well, he didn't make any sign that he'd been offended, but a minute or two later I heard a little commotion outside the restaurant and stepped out. Those two travelers were down on the platform, dead to the world. The lumberjack, packsack on his back, was going calmly up the spur track to Hunter's Mill.

Or listen to a wizened old woods foreman, Tom Francis, as he studies the stub of his cigar and haltingly relishes his youthful role of northwoods Lochinvar:

I was comin' up on the train to Newberry. This big gaffer got on at Trout Lake ... mebbe he'd had a few - I don't know. Anyway ... conductor was in another car an' this geezer started throwin' his weight around ... car was full of women an' he got talkin' pretty rank ... struttin' up an' down like a cock partridge ... way outa line, y'know. I wasn't askin' for no trouble, not in a place like that, anyhow, but about the third time by an' give me a nudge, why, I was set for him. I got the best leverage I could in that damn seat - an' I peeled him one ... must've slid him half the length of the car. That ended that. (A little deprecatory chuckle, and then:) You should've seen the way those women made over me! I guess that day the Good Lord's overcoat wouldn't'a made me a vest!

Always there lurked danger. It watched from the heaped-up rollways, lurked in the crowns of trees, mocked the top-loader's catlike agility, and dogged the canthook men "sending up" to him. When a log "cannoned" it slipped from the confining chain and slid endwise. In its lethal potentiality if it shot toward you it was well named.

Diverse in their origins, Tahquamenon woodsmen gained a kind of stark homogeneity on the roster of accidental death. Many names were added in my time, though the day of pine was long past; some of them I remember well. Erick Jacobson, the kindly Swede who with saw and hand-plane could shape pine or oak into cabinetry with a skill that challenged the eye to find the joining, crawled wretchedly from beneath the mill where he had tried to shove a belt onto a spoked pulley with a stick,

Horse skidding, 1968, with Willard Hines, Michigan Pole and Tie Company, Taylor woods, Hulbert.

with only breath enough to whisper, "I gutted myself." The crew waited in horror for the car that would take him out of sight - but never out of mind. Tracy Reed was clean-killed by a falling limb. In his veins coursed the old Anglo-Saxon stream that had invigorated the settlers of the Appalachians of Kentucky and the Virginias. A rifleman, and a good one, he carried half an armful of pieces with him when he moved from place to place in the valley. Seen now in the boyhood mirror of foretime, they shine. I see Bonneau, famed for the size of his log-loads, boring down M-123 "with his foot in the carburetor." Men of his lineage, two generations removed, had danced lightly on brown lids of logs in water. One evening his long luck broke. Canthook freed, a front stake on his truck whipped savagely. ("Bound fast ... must have been," they said.) Soon he was in the Tall Timber. Then, among others, Daniel Bird. Aloof and proud - proud of his Chippewa forebears - Dan had played football with the great Thorpe at Carlisle Institute. Home again in the deep woods of his people, he chopped and sawed at the white man's trees, and remained disdainful of all this civilization except the white man's Bible. He was crisped one night in his burning shack, his little black dog beside him.

   Dr. F. P. Bohn of Newberry, who knew the lumberjack well,

described him this way: "He had a rough exterior and a heart of gold. He could out-drink and out-fight any other class of humanity I have ever seen and he went about all of his activities lustily with a pride in accomplishment. To the man who treated him fairly and gave him square dealing and square friendship, he was a square dealer and a square friend."

But mainly what we saw was a special sort of workman, schooled in what are now forgotten, outmoded skills, remembered in the guise of lumberjack, logger or woodsman. Perhaps, if we are heartwise, we shall let his memory be, for he has no need, anymore than the Daniel Boones or Kit Carsons of our other frontiers ever had, for the sentimental effrontery that would pry him loose from the embedded roots of our folklore, and jackstraw him into a grotesque caricature of mythic size.

YACHTING.ON THE.TAQUOMENON
NEWBERRY MICH

Postscript:
Vignettes of Northern Life

The Riddle of "McGruer's Gods"

John McGruer may not have known much about archaeology, but one day in the year 1896 this Newberry farmer had his name linked with an unearthing that not only set townspeople agog, but also caused reverberations of curiosity and wonder to echo throughout the state.

Time has dealt in its usual way with McGruer and all the wonderment about the curious "idols" that came from his woodlot. But it has not, apparently, served to solve very much of the mystery of their finding. Nor has it appeared to lessen, in the minds of the few who still recall the event or its aftermath, the conviction that neither McGruer nor anyone associated with him was capable of perpetrating such a hoax.

It all began, people said, when McGruer sent two local lumberjacks, John Gordon and George Howe, out to cut wood

Sprague Taylor

Remains of tablet, 1947.

for him on a forty he owned a mile west of the Four Mile Corner, north of the village.

Essentially, the story they returned with was that while putting up wood, they saw a stray mink and chased it beneath the roots of an upturned hemlock. Peering underneath, they saw part of the exposed head of what seemed to be a crude sandstone statue. Quickly digging it out - and breaking it into several pieces in their haste, for it proved later to be of hardened clay - they poked nearby and unearthed two more statues, together with a slab, or tablet, of the same material.

And so into Newberry they hurried, weighted down with certainly as strange a result of mink-chasing as ever turned up in a northwoods village.

News of the find spread quickly, and souvenir hunters descended on the woodlot site by the wagonload. Nothing more, so far as can be learned, was ever found.

For several weeks the images, set up on display in Newberry, caused widespread speculation. The largest was nearly four feet in height and, according to one observer, had been formed in a sitting posture. The next in size was standing, and the smallest, thought to represent a child, was a little less than two feet long.

Weird as these supposed artifacts were, it was the tablet that caused most of the excitement. About eighteen by twenty-four

Sprague Taylor

The head of the largest image, 1947.

inches in size, it had one surface divided into 140 squares, each of which contained an undecipherable character.

Puzzled eyes focused hard on these tablet symbols. Clergymen dusted off volumes of ancient history that illustrated, some said, resemblances between the strange markings and Egyptian hieroglyphics - or letters of the Greek alphabet. A prominent lumberman, not to be outshone by men of the cloth, gave it as his opinion that McGruer's men had happened upon an ancient calendar. Either that, he declared, or a gameboard of some sort, resembling our checkers.

In all the furor that resulted, there is no indication that McGruer, or the workmen Gordon and Howe, or a local jeweler, L. N. Forbes, who was said to be "interested in the ownership" with McGruer, ever made any quotable comments on their good fortune. By this silence they seemed to be saying that they had brought the things to light by happy accident; they were as mystified as anyone about their origin or significance; and they awaited whatever scientific judgment of the day might be forthcoming.

Here they differed markedly from the relic peddlers who operated in the Lower Peninsula, especially near Detroit, in the following two decades, who tested public gullibility with

Sprague Taylor

Remains of the middle-sized image, 1947.

everything from copies of Noah's diary to prehistoric beer mugs.

Clearly, no hint of connivance came into local print. Charles Brebner, editor of *The Newberry News* at the time, took a dim view of pranksters, whether they were announcing bloody attacks on woodsmen by timber wolves, or, more innocently, reporting the capture of a seventeen-foot "sea monster" in Muskallonge Lake. He described the find as "one of the wonders of the age," sent photographs of the collection to the Smithsonian Institution in Washington, and published a reply indicating an inability to deliver an immediate opinion on authenticity, and asking for more details.

Gradually the stir died down. John McGruer stored his unusual property in his barn on the bank of the Tahquamenon. Occasionally, in the thirty years of forgetfulness that followed, local youngsters would interrupt their swimming hole fun to sneak in and take a furtive look at what had come to be known as "McGruer's gods."

Then, about 1929, some of the fragments that remained were pieced together and taken to St. Ignace for display in a small museum, Fort Algonquin, owned by H. Vaughn Norton. Further deteriorated, they were later moved to another St. Ignace museum, Fort de Baude.

Was, indeed, the whole thing nothing more than an engaging hoax?

Obviously so, some present-day archaeologists have said, studying the figures and the tablet - or photographs of them.

Not necessarily so, said some older residents, questioned at length in the late 1940's. They had seen the find in 1896; they remembered it well; and to them there remained a certain irrefutable logic in their unanimous assessment of the finders: "They simply weren't ingenious enough to think it up."

Very possibly true, but also true appears to be the fact that somebody may have displayed a considerable knack for straight-faced tomfoolery - and got away with it.

If there is any last word, it remains a postscript elusively hidden. Or perhaps it was said, once and for all, in a sly comment in the *Detroit Journal*, shortly after the state first heard about it. William Jennings Bryan, of oratorical fame, had just been hotly pursuing the presidency. The Detroit writer allowed that while the untranslatable markings on the McGruer tablet could not possibly be one of the golden-tongued Bryan's campaign speeches set to music he found it "hard to keep one's mind and the suggestion wide apart."

excerpted from
The Mining Journal (Marquette)
February 10, 1966

Harry Hart

The brief item in The Newberry News *began: "Harry H. Hart died November 19, 1971, at his home." Five years earlier I had taken my camera and paid him a visit in his isolated dwelling, because it seemed to me that he, with his reclusive disposition, typified a special kind of old-time woodsman. He was seventy-nine at that time. An account of the visit follows.*

Deep in the lowland that has come to be known as the Great Tahquamenon Swamp, Harry Hart keeps a calendar on the door of the little camp where he lives alone, about ten miles from Newberry.

Recently, instead of marking in the usual "x" to set off the passing of another date, Hart entered the single word "town."

Eighty-three quiet winter days had slipped by since he had last made - a short while before Christmas - a similar notation.

Going out to town means a ten-mile hike, and Hart, who has always preferred to go it alone, is in his 80th year. This time, for a change, he accepted a ride.

In Newberry for his first trip to the outside world in nearly three months, he laughed a little when people in the business section, used to his solitary ways, told him they had been getting worried about him. Then he went about his brief errands.

Sprague Taylor

Harry Hart.

He picked up his mail at the Post Office. He chatted with his friend Bill Johnson, the druggist who owns the land his camp is on, and gathered up a stack of magazines and newspapers. Though he was far from out of food, he added to his provisions with two boxes of canned goods.

Another longtime friend, Joe Rahilly, gave him a lift back. At the trail leading away from the highway, Hart put his purchases on a sled and went back home.

Once, Bill Johnson recalls, he suggested to Hart that he might be happier if he had a place closer to the road. The reply that came back - along with a grin - was direct:

"I'm too close now."

Ask about Harry Hart around Newberry, and you will learn chiefly the details of his infrequent appearances. The town has known three generations of woodsmen, and his sort of self-sufficiency, if unusual now, is not new.

You may learn that in the years when he used to outfit at McMillan, west of here, the storekeepers there spoke of him as "the gentleman lumberjack." Apparently, in an era of much casual boisterousness, he stood out because of his reserve and neatness of dress.

If, in a time when the loneliness of the aged is a problem of growing concern, you turn delicately to the subject with Hart, he shrugs and says briefly:

"I like it this way."

He reveals that during World War II, while he was still working, he once spent three months on a job as a cutter - and did not see a person for the duration. Now an occasional bobcat hunter or ski-sledder stops by.

Although he chooses to live by himself, he is not without woodland company. Deer and bear have a way of becoming tame at his camp, and partridges and rabbits, too, as if sensing that the guns hanging neatly above his bunk will not be leveled at them. In turn, Hart has a way of discouraging the rare game violator who happens down his trail.

For most of his life, you find, he made his living with axe and saw. When pressed a trifle to tell about the scenes he has known, he will glance at you inquiringly, but not unkindly, as if to find it strange that anyone should wonder about time that is gone - or ranks that have thinned. Matter-of-factly they return - the products, the places, the people.

He has hewn railroad ties by the thousands with a broadaxe ("Once we got a dime for the big ones, a nickel for the small ones."), peeled hemlock tanbark, cut cedar fence posts, felled white pine for lumber, and piled up spruce and balsam pulpwood by uncounted cords.

There were the outfitting places - McMillan, Newberry, Trout Lake - and the temporary shipping points on the railroads like Hendrie on the old South Shore, or Dick and Mile 49 on the Soo Line. He saw them all.

The names of lumbermen he knew or worked for - Hunter, Madden, Wood, Furlong, McLeod, Chesbrough, and in particular his good friend of recent years, Jack Hyde - come back like a roster of a fraternity known the length and breadth of the broad valley the Tahquamenon forms.

Born near Sarnia, Ontario, Hart watched hewers of wood in

action as a boy. Now, broadaxe set aside, he can reflect on other timber he has seen. Giant cedar and redwood in British Columbia and California, during a youthful wandering. Shellbroken beeches in the Argonne Forest, during World War I.

But most of all, he remembers the variety of trees he once moved among in the neck of the woods he calls home, when his work made islands of sound and the chips flew bright from the cut.

This is not to say that he lives in the past. He is an avid reader, especially of the Sunday editions of *The New York Times*.

And if he runs out?

"I start over," he says. "It's surprising what you miss the first time through."

Once he confided, "You never really know the woods until you listen to the sounds of it at night."

And so he lives with the night sounds, apart by choice from the kind of world where men often look for contentment in the crowd, or in the stir of daily events.

Harry Hart has always liked it his way.

excerpted from
The Evening News (Sault Ste. Marie)
March 30, 1966

The Foundering of the *Cyprus*

For more than sixty years there were lifesavers stationed along the Lake Superior edge of Luce County at Crisp Point, the mouth of the Two Hearted River, and Deer Park. Now and then, in a bygone time of navigation that knew neither radio nor radar, the wires that connected these remote stations with the outside world of landsmen carried terse and tragic messages.

Such a dispatch came from Deer Park Life Saving Station No. 12, as it was then called, early in the morning of October 12, 1907. One of its crewmen, reported later to be Ralph Ocea, had been on solitary beach patrol a half-mile east of the station. A gale, which had come up the previous day, blew from the northwest. At about 2:00 a.m. he heard faint cries for help, and in the dim light of his lantern, he located a man, helpless from exposure, lying beside a life raft.

The sailor was Charles J. Pitz, second mate and sole survivor of a crew of twenty-three aboard the freighter *Cyprus*. Revived at Deer Park, Pitz told a harrowing story.

Launched at Lorain, Ohio, on September 17, 1907, the
***Cyprus* has one of the shortest careers of any "laker"—25**
days.

The *Cyprus* had been downbound the day before from
Superior, Wisconsin, with slightly over 7,000 tons of iron in her
hold. The storm, though severe, was the kind that many similar
ships had often been able to ride out to safety. But she apparently
took on water through her unbattened hatches. About 18 miles
off Deer Park, the immense cargo shifted, and she developed a
bad list to port. Soon she could no longer be kept under way.
Fires in the engine room were reported out at 7:35 p.m.

With little time to prepare to abandon ship, Captain F. B. Huyck
called out, "It's all off, boys"; and with Pitz, the first mate and
a watchman, stood by the pilot house life raft. The others under
his command tried desperately to launch boats near the stern.
At 7:45 p.m. the *Cyprus* sank in 300 feet of water.

Above the sound of the wind, the four men clinging to the raft
could hear the shouts of other crewmen, soon silenced by the
waves. Then began their own brutal, six-hour struggle for
survival.

Driven shoreward, the four tried to help each other hold to
the lines of the raft. They were washed off repeatedly. First Mate
J. N. Smith weakened, lost his grip, and drowned. Watchman
George Thorn developed a cramp from submersion in the icy
water. Soon he, too, was gone. Before reaching the tremendous
off-beach surf, Captain Huyck gave his watch to Pitz, asking
weakly that it be sent to his wife.

J.V. Kinsey

Raft of sole survivor of the *Cyprus*, washed ashore a half mile east of Deer Park, 1907.

"As we neared the shore," Pitz was quoted as saying later, "the raft turned over time after time." Somehow he managed to remain with it. Then he was conscious only that he had been flung on the sand, and that he was alone. He had, he said, an unwavering conviction that he would make it; and when he saw Ocea's lantern coming up to him through the gloom, it appeared to glow like some great swinging ball of fire.

Within a day or two, nineteen bodies were found along a twelve-mile stretch of shore. To add poignancy to an already bleak scene, one of them was that of a young woman, the wife of Steward William Dundon. She had worked aboard the *Cyprus*, beside her husband, as second cook.

Pitz continued to sail the lakes, including the one that nearly claimed his life; and in marine circles, his ordeal by water became one of the legendary sagas of survival on the inland seas.

excerpted from
The Newberry News
February 17, 1966

Epilogue

From Sprague Taylor's Journal, 10/25/45

I sat, not long ago, on the top of the winding stairway which goes up the center of the 100-foot fire tower at McNearney Lake, my purpose being to catch the elusive rays of the sun if they happened to break through the clouds and furnish light for a picture of the lake. Though on the ground there was but a mild breeze from the north, up there it seemed that a gale swept about the thin girders and cross pieces, making me choose my grip and my footing deliberately. I did not have a chance to use the camera, even though I waited fully half an hour and felt a numbness creeping into my fingers, but the experience was unusual and exhilarating. About me on three sides the reaches of land were visible for about fifteen miles: northward across Tahquamenon Bay I could see the tip of Whitefish Point curving into the lake, and farther east, the heights of Canada, across the entrance to the St. Marys. The town of Eckerman stood out plainly against the southwest horizon, and smoke could be seen rising from Sheldon's mill. Farther west, across the swamp, bisected by the old Cadillac grade, bands of sunlight shot through clouds suddenly rifted and lay down upon the timbered hills a shifting streak of gold. Through the rain squall hanging over the bay I could now and then catch a glimpse of freighters, their smoke swept from stacks by the rushing wind, and swept low across the water. And for nearly all the while I was perched there, huddled in a mackinaw against the cold, a pair of bald eagles kept a swooping, circling vigil over the lake. Once, thinking that they had left the scene, I was surprised to have them reappear from the valley at my rear, to sweep low across the end of the lake at close range—close enough, at any rate, that their white markings were very plain. No wonder, I thought then, that the flight of an eagle has been associated with freedom. Now hunting close together, now separated by half a mile, they soared in an uninhabited fastness all their own, up and down, at times hovering almost motionless far above my head, then circling still upward in great spirals, until, nearly nothing but dots lost in the cloud bank, they glided gracefully earthward, only to repeat the process time and again. There was the wind; there was the scudding of clouds above a vista of wooded heights and valleys. There were the eagles. Could I, in that half hour, have asked for more?

Bibliographical Essay

Most comprehensive accounts of activities in the Lake Superior region (missionary life, the fur trade, lumbering, fishing, etc.) have been prepared by persons intent on wider perspectives. In general, those seeking to learn the story of the Tahquamenon country, especially the record which precedes the pine lumbering era, must assemble information from brief remarks contained in a large and scattered assortment of diverse materials.

For help in locating certain written and illustrative material I am indebted to the staffs of a number of libraries and agencies, and notably to those of the public library of Sault Ste. Marie, Michigan; the Marquette County Historical Society and the Bishop Baraga Association, both of Marquette; the Burton Historical Collection of the Detroit Public Library; the Michigan Historical Commission Archives, Lansing; Clarke Historical Library, Central Michigan University, Mount Pleasant; the

Michigan Historical Collections and the Clements Library, University of Michigan, Ann Arbor; the Grand Rapids Public Library; the Office of County Register of Deeds at Sault Ste. Marie and also at Newberry, and the Upper Peninsula Branch of the Michigan State Library, Escanaba. I am also obliged on the same account to the American Baptist Foreign Mission Society, New York City; the National Archives, Washington, D. C.; the State Historical Society of Wisconsin, Madison; the Forest History Society, New Haven, Connecticut; and the Douglas Library, Queen's University, Kingston, Ontario.

Bibliography

This list contains the written sources, of both primary and secondary significance, most frequently used to prepare this book.

BOOKS

Adney, E. T. & Chapelle, H. I. **The Bark Canoes and Skin Boats of North America.** Washington, D.C.: Smithsonian Institution, 1964.

Bergquist, Stannard G. **The Pleistocene History of the Tahquamenon and Manistique Drainage Region of the Northern Peninsula of Michigan**. Lansing, Michigan, 1936.

Calvin, D. D. **A Saga of the St. Lawrence**. Toronto, Ontario: The Ryerson Press, 1945.

Commission of Indian Affairs. **Treaties Between the United States of America and the Several Indian Tribes from 1778 to 1837**. Washington, D.C., 1837.

Dollar, Robert. **Memoirs**. San Francisco, California, 1917. 2v. [Volume 1 has an account of the founding of Dollarville, Michigan.]

Flatt, William D. **The Trail of Love**. Toronto, Ontario: Briggs, 1916. [Copy read at Douglas Library, Queen's University, Kingston, Ontario.]

Gilman, C. R. **Life on the Lakes**.

New York, New York, 1836. 2v.
Hinsdale, Wilbert B.
Archaeological Atlas of Michigan. Ann Arbor, Michigan, 1931.
Hotchkiss, George W. **History of the Lumber and Forest Industry of the Northwest**. Chicago, Illinois, 1898.
Hulbert, W. D. **Forest Neighbors**. New York, New York, 1902.
_____. **White Pine Days on the Tahquamenon**. Lansing, Michigan: Historical Society of Michigan, 1949.
Kappler, Charles J., editor. **Indian Affairs, Laws and Treaties**. Washington, D.C., 1904.
Kohl, J. K. **Kitchi-Gami: Wanderings Round Lake Superior**. Minneapolis, Minnesota: Ross & Haines, Inc., 1956.
Masson, L. R. **Les bourgeois de la compagnie du nord-ouest**. Quebec, 1889. 2v. [Volume 1 contains "An Account of Lake Superior, 1792-1807," by John Johnston, Sault Ste. Marie fur trader.]
McIntosh, Robert W. "Wildland Planning Procedures. . . in the Tahquamenon - Pictured Rocks Region, Upper Peninsula of Michigan." Unpublished Ph.D. dissertation, University of Michigan, Ann Arbor, 1955.
McKenney, Thomas L. **Sketches of a Tour to the Lakes**. Baltimore, Maryland, 1827.
_____ and Hall, James. **The Indian Tribes of North America**. Edinburgh, Scotland, 1933. 3v.
Newberry State Hospital. **Propositions of Local Committees Offering Sites of an Asylum for the Insane**. Lansing, Michigan, n.d.
Noblet, U.J. **Forest Trees of the Tahquamenon River Region and the Upper Peninsula of**

Michigan. Newberry, Michigan: Tahquamenon River Boat Service, n.d.
Pitezel, John H. **Life of Peter Marksman**. Cincinnati, Ohio, 1893.
_____. **Lights and Shades of Missionary Life**. Cincinnati, Ohio, 1882.
Quimby, George I. **Indian Life in the Upper Great Lakes 11,000 B.C. to A.D. 1800**. Chicago, Illinois, 1960.
Rezek, A.I. **History of the Diocese of Sault Ste. Marie and Marquette**. Houghton, Michigan, 1906.
Sawyer, Alvah H. **Northern Peninsula of Michigan**. Chicago, Illinois, 1911. 2v.
Schoolcraft, H.R. **Historical and Statistical Information Respecting. . . the Indian Tribes of the United States**. Philadelphia, Pennsylvania, 1851-1857. 6v.
_____. **Oneota, or, Characteristics of the Red Race of America**. New York, New York, 1845.
_____. **Personal Memoirs of a Residence of Thirty Years with the Indian Tribes. . . .** Philadelphia, Pennsylvania, 1851.
Shaffmaster, A.D. **Hunting in the Land of Hiawatha, or the Hunting Trips of an Editor**. Chicago, Illinois, 1904.
St. Gregory's Parish, Diamond Jubilee, 1886-1961. Newberry, Michigan.
Thwaites, R.G., editor. **The Jesuit Relations**. Cleveland, Ohio, 1896-1901. 73v. [Volumes 53 and 54, chiefly, were consulted.]
Warren, William W. **History of the Ojibway Nation**. (Volume 5 of the Collections of the Minnesota Historical Society) St. Paul, Minnesota, 1885.

PERIODICALS

Bohn, Dr. Frank P. "This Was the Forest Primeval," **Michigan History Magazine**, 21 (1937), 21-38; 170-196.

Caister, Daniel. "The Historical Occupation at Naomikong Point." Research paper, Museum of Anthropology, University of Michigan, 1968.

Deasy, George F. "Agriculture in Luce County, Michigan 1880 to 1930," **Agricultural History**, 24 (January, 1950), 1-4.

Dodge, Charles K. "Observations on the Wild Plants at Whitefish Point and Vermilion . . . and Other Parts of Chippewa County, Michigan, in 1914," **Michigan Geological and Biological Survey**, Publication 33 (1921), 125-164.

The Evening News, Sault Ste. Marie, Michigan

Hulbert, R. C. "Pioneers at Hulbert," **Michigan History Magazine**, 31 (June, 1947), 174-191.

Janzen, Donald E. "The Naomikong Point Site and the Dimensions of Laurel in the Lake Superior Region," Anthropological Papers, Museum of Anthropology, University of Michigan, Ann Arbor. No. 36, 1968.

Northwestern Lumberman. Chicago, Illinois, 1873-1898. (The years 1878-1898 are in the Peter White Library, Marquette, Michigan.)

Railway 7 Locomotive Society Bulletin, No. 111, Duluth, South Shore & Atlantic.

Quimby, George I. "Exploring an Underwater Indian Site," **Chicago Natural History Museum Bulletin**, 36 (November 8, 1965), 2-4.

Spring, Ida M. "White Pine Portraits," a series of articles on Tahquamenon country lumbermen published in **Michigan History Magazine**: Big Dave Ranson, 31 (September, 1947), 314-321; Con Culhane, 31 (December, 1947), 437-442; "Genial" Dan McLeod, 30 (Jan-Mar., 1946), 59-72; "Norwegian" Jack Ryland, 32 (September, 1948), 295-300.

ARCHIVAL SOURCES

Anthony, James H. Twelve letters written to Peter B. Barbeau of Sault Ste. Marie from James Pendill's "Carp River Saw Mill" in 1857. Marquette County Historical Society, Marquette, Michigan.

Barbeau, Peter B. Diaries and letters. Marquette County Historical Society, Marquette, Michigan.

Bingham, Abel. Thirty-eight diaries and journals and about 2,500 letters. Clarke Historical Library, Central Michigan University, Mount Pleasant, Michigan.

_____. Letters between 1828 and 1855. American Baptist Foreign Mission Society, New York City, New York.

_____. Annual reports to agents of the Office of Indian Affairs. National Archives in Washington D. C.

_____. Journals, 1829-1840. Grand Rapids Public Library, Grand Rapids, Michigan.

_____. Diaries, account books, sermons and family letters. Michigan Historical Collections, University of Michigan, Ann Arbor, Michigan.

Burt, William A. Fifteen letters to the Surveyor General of the Northwest, 1840-1841, National Archives, Washington, D.C.

_____. Survey Records. Original field books and plats. Marquette County Historical

Society, Marquette, Michigan.

Burt, Wells. Field Notes. Notes of his subdivisional surveys, 1849-1850. Office of the Chippewa County Surveyor, Sault Ste. Marie, Michigan, and the office of the Luce County Clerk, Newberry, Michigan.

Calvin & Breck, Quebec. Letterbooks and papers (in particular those to do with logging of board timber in Tahquamenon area from 1876 to 1879). Douglas Library, Queen's University, Kingston, Ontario.

Cameron, James D. Correspondence, 1832-1859. American Foreign Mission Society, New York City, New York.

_____. Correspondence directed to Abel Bingham, Sault Ste. Marie. Clarke Historical Library, Central Michigan University, Mount Pleasant, Michigan.

Franchere, Gabriel. A letterpress book, American Fur Company, Sault Ste. Marie, Michigan, 1835-1838. Bayliss Library, Sault Ste. Marie, Michigan.

Hulbert, R. C. Correspondence, 1945-1951. Reminiscences of the Tahquamenon pine era. Author's collection.

Johnston, George. Ledger. Burton Historical Collection, Detroit Public Library, Detroit, Michigan.

Lawrence, H. C. Correspondence, 1947-1951. Letters on Tahqua-menon surveys. Author's collection.

McMillan, James. Papers. Records on the Duluth, South Shore & Atlantic Railway Company, 1880's. Burton Historical Collection, Detroit Public Library, Detroit, Michigan.

Michigan Pioneer and Historical Collections. Lansing, Michigan, 1874-1915.

Newberry State Hospital. Minutes and reports 1895-1926. Michigan State Archives, Lansing, Michigan.

Pendill, James P. Inventory, 1854. (A list of property held at his Pendill's Creek sawmill) Bayliss Library, Sault Ste. Marie, Michigan.

Pitezel, John H. Diaries. Personal notebooks on the Naomikong mission, and other missionary work on Whitefish Bay. Clarke Historical Library, Central Michigan University, Mount Pleasant, Michigan.

Schoolcraft, H. R. Letter Book. Outgoing correspondence, Office of Indian Affairs, Sault Ste. Marie, 1822-1833. National Archives, Washington D.C.

_____. The Literary Voyageur. . . . A manuscript periodical, 1826-1827. Photostatic copies of some issues are in the Michigan Historical Collections, University of Michigan, Ann Arbor, Michigan.

Index

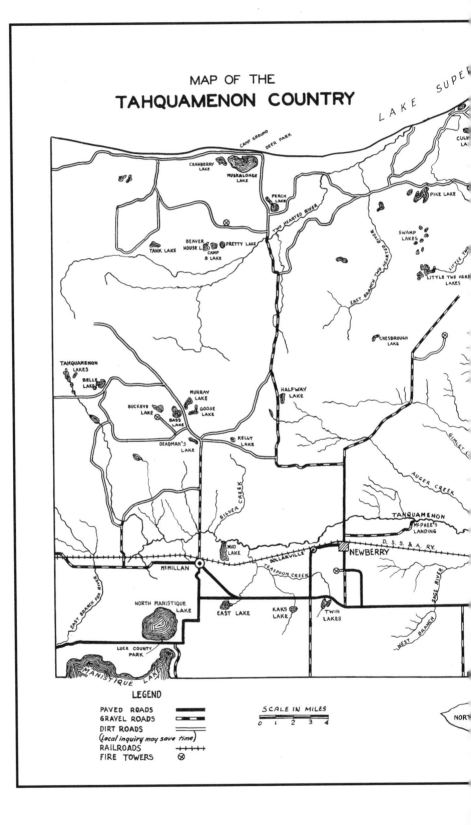

MAP OF THE
TAHQUAMENON COUNTRY

LAKE SUPE

CAMP GROUND
DEER PARK
CRANBERRY LAKE
MUSKALONGE LAKE
CULK LAKE
PIKE LAKE
PERCH LAKE
SWAMP LAKES
TWO HEARTED RIVER
LITTLE TWO
EAST BRANCH TWO HEARTED RIVER
LITTLE TWO HEAD LAKES
BEAVER HOUSE L.
PRETTY LAKE
TANK LAKE
CAMP B LAKE
CHESBROUGH LAKE
TAHQUAMENON LAKES
BELLE LAKE
MURRAY LAKE
GOOSE LAKE
BUCKEYE LAKE
BASS LAKE
HALFWAY LAKE
GIMLET C.
DEADMAN'S LAKE
KELLY LAKE
AUGER CREEK
SILVER CREEK
TAHQUAMENON
McPHEE'S LANDING
MUD LAKE
DOLLARVILLE
D. S. S. & A. RY.
NEWBERRY
McMILLAN
TEASPOON CREEK
EAST BRANCH FOX RIVER
NORTH MANISTIQUE LAKE
EAST LAKE
KAKS LAKE
TWIN LAKES
EAGLE RIVER
WEST BRANCH
LUCE COUNTY PARK
MANISTIQUE LA
NOR

LEGEND

PAVED ROADS	▬▬▬
GRAVEL ROADS	▬ ▭ ▬
DIRT ROADS	─────
(Local inquiry may save time)	
RAILROADS	┼┼┼┼┼
FIRE TOWERS	⊗

SCALE IN MILES
0   1   2   3   4

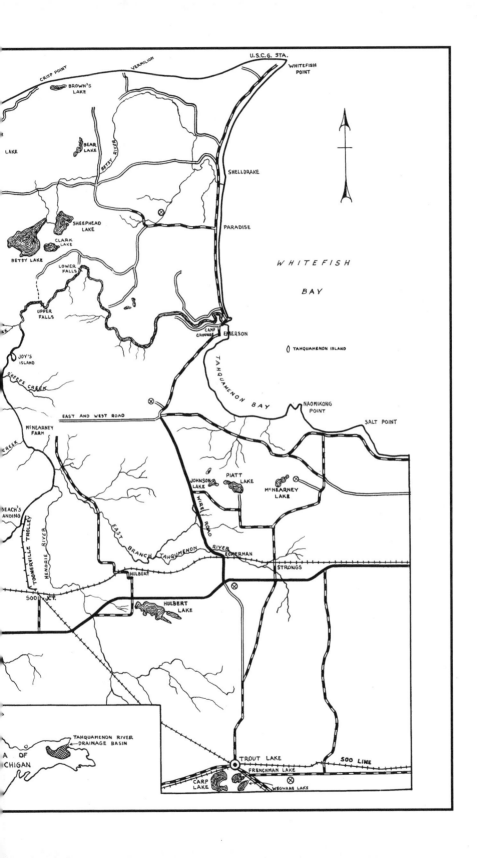